Intercession & Healing

ELLEL MINISTRIES
THE TRUTH & FREEDOM SERIES

Intercession & Healing

Breaking through with God

Fiona Horrobin

Sovereign World

Sovereign World Ltd
Ellel Grange
Bay Horse
Lancaster
Lancashire LA2 0HN
United Kingdom

www.sovereignworld.com

ISBN 978 1 85240 500 7

The publishers aim to produce books which will help to extend and build up the Kingdom of God. We do not necessarily agree with every view expressed by the authors, or with every interpretation of Scripture expressed. We expect readers to make their own judgment in the light of their understanding of God's Word and in an attitude of Christian love and fellowship.

Cover design by Andy Taylor
Typeset by Hurix Systems Pvt. Limited

Contents

Confidentiality

The stories and illustrations in this book have been disguised to protect the identity of individuals. They are written in a way which amalgamates a number of similar stories and experiences.

Dedication

With loving thanks to my husband, children, team members and those whose lives have touched the pages of this book. Without you, I wouldn't be the person I am and I couldn't have written in the way I have. May all the glory, honor and praise go to the Lord Jesus who is the giver of life.

Foreword

This is a fantastic book. It's full of practical insights to help those of us who are praying for others and longing for them to be healed. Have you prayed, yet seen little change? Have you wished God would heal, and believed He can, yet been frustrated by the limits you keep bumping up against? Perhaps there are different ways to pray which would help. Perhaps you wish you could pray effectively with the person you love, or the people in your church who need help, but you don't know what to say. If your heart is longing for God to show you what else you could say or do, that's probably the reason He has put this book into your hands.

Fiona Horrobin has a wealth of experience. She also has a huge heart of love and compassion. Someone once described her to me like this, "Fiona's amazing. I have never seen anyone whose eyes radiate so much love." As Paul says, *'if I have all knowledge, and if I have a faith that can move mountains, but have not love, I am nothing'* (1 Corinthians 13:2). Fiona has love and she also has faith and knowledge. What a combination! May God's blessing overflow through you to others as you apply the insights in this book.

Dr. Grace Marshall

Preface

Prayer is a broad subject and there are many wonderful books written on it. This book is not a comprehensive scriptural overview of intercession, rather it's designed to encourage, inspire and equip those who want to see the kingdom of God grow on earth, using ordinary people in ordinary ways.

Jesus speaks to His disciples saying, *"Do not be afraid, little flock, for it is your Father's good pleasure to give you the kingdom"* (Luke 12:32). He also speaks to them saying, *"I will give you the keys of the kingdom of heaven, and whatever you bind on earth will be bound in heaven, and whatever you loose on earth will be loosed in heaven"* (Matthew 16:19).

The work of the kingdom embraces all who are disciples of the Lord Jesus Christ. Included in this book are helpful insights and powerful keys for seeing change through answers to your prayers. It's designed to help those who want to be 'naturally supernatural' (1 Corinthians 1:26-31). God uses the weak and foolish things of this world to turn the world's wisdom upside down. God the Father turns the ideas and ways of men around so that He can bring about His purposes. Our Triune God (Father, Son and Holy Spirit) has ways and thoughts which are far above our ways (Isaiah 55:8-9).

It's beyond our understanding that this infinite, all-powerful God who created the heavens and the earth invites us to join with Him in the incredible adventure of ushering in His eternal purposes. He seeks our participation and partnership on His journey and incredibly He has bound Himself to us in unbreakable (covenantal) love throughout it all. He's our Father and we are His children and His greatest desire is for us to share in His inheritance to us.

This book aims to open up some of the contents of God's box of treasures. It's illustrated with stories drawn from over twenty years of experience of adventuring with Him in the healing ministry. It illustrates something of the relationship between the human and the divine. It will encourage you to place your life afresh into the hands of your Maker and allow Him to fashion who you are, in order to bring about His eternal purposes.

Intensely practical, this book's intended as a guide for those who want to see the power of God released in such a way that it will bring about changes in the spiritual climate, which in turn affects the earthly climate. It's about doing our part in participating with God to reach those in need. He will then do His part. He will bring about the change, remove the obstacle, break the bondage, heal the sick, and bind up the broken hearted.

Our life is a prayer. When it's laid down in its fallibility and human-ness, the miracle is that God brings about a miracle of divine multiplication. The challenge of this book is to allow God to use you to be a channel of His grace and mercy. He's not looking for the perfect person or a superstar, but He *is* looking for a willing person. When He has a person who desires to be His heart, hands and feet to others, there's no telling what He's able to accomplish.

Journeying with God is not about our qualifications, our experience, our professionalism or our adequacy. At the heart of this book is my desire to encourage all who think of themselves as 'clay pots' in the master's hand. Our Heavenly Father longs to take all that we are and all that we offer to Him, and reveal the keys of His kingdom in the realm of prayer. He does this so that He can bring in His kingdom purposes here on earth.

What a challenge this is to us who are ordinary folk desiring to be obedient to the One who has given us life in Jesus. Do we believe that God can and will use us if we allow Him to? I pray this book will cause you to find yourself on a new page in your understanding and effectiveness in the works of the kingdom. More than that, I pray your life will be turned into an ongoing prayer, and become a garden of beautiful fruit, borne out of a life touched by the Maker.

As you turn the pages, you will find keys, stories, illustrations and insights which will help you enter into the active place God has for you in His kingdom.

Jesus taught us, *"Pray then this way; Our Father in heaven, hallowed be your name. Your kingdom come. Your will be done, on earth as it is in heaven"* (Matthew 6:9-10). This gives us the pattern and challenges us to be part of the answer. I pray you will be inspired and helped into greater fruitfulness and blessing in the work of the Kingdom of God today.

Fiona Horrobin
Ellel Grange, October 2008

Introduction

An ordinary day – I was walking towards my work at the office, when it all changed as I heard loud screams coming from a public toilet. I shuddered at the thought of what might be wrong. Maybe someone was having a baby, or a miscarriage, or had been stabbed, or something else that was terrible. My imagination ran riot in the moment that it took me to decide to speed up my walk and reach the office as soon as possible.

I was in my late teens at the time and had always hated anything to do with operations or blood. My natural instinct was to go the other way if there were accidents. But this time was different. As I passed by, I felt a deep conviction in my heart. Would I just ignore those screams and leave the person in trouble without help?

With my heart beating and knees knocking, I returned to the toilet entrance. By now quite a few people had gathered around. I quietly asked a lady nearby whether anyone had gone to the person inside. I hoped that they had and I would be absolved from doing anything further. However, this wasn't the case and I found myself saying, "If I go to help, will you come with me?" Her answer was, "yes."

We both walked down the stairwell into the toilets which were situated in a car park. The sobbing and screaming was becoming louder. My imagination was running riot but I managed to say in a loud voice, "it's all right. We've come to help you." Almost before the words had come off my tongue, the door of the toilet was flung wide open and into my arms fell a girl as young as myself.

"Oh thank you, thank you," she sobbed as she hung onto me for dear life. She was extremely distressed and finally was able to tell us what had happened. It turned out that a 'peeping tom' (a man intent on viewing women in a naked or semi-naked condition without permission) had climbed over the top of the toilet to view her.

My overwhelming emotion was relief that it was nothing worse, no blood or stabbing! I was happy to have helped the lady and as we parted, she spoke the words, "thank you for rescuing me."

This incident was to stay with me for the rest of my life. In many ways, it was a very ordinary incident. However, it was the time when God made me aware that I could walk on in line with my natural instincts and desires, or I could trust Him to take me out of my comfort zone and into His purposes. I had great joy in rescuing the lady in the toilet.

That experience was a bit like the story of the Good Samaritan in Luke chapter 10, where three people had walked by a wounded man lying on the road and only one had stopped to care. The others all had excuses. God doesn't want onlookers in His kingdom. He longs for those who will walk with him and be part of the answer with Him. This is the essence of intercession and I had a lot to learn in my journey!

Early background

Coming from a strong evangelical Christian background, prayer was part of our family life. My parents were in many ways very ordinary people. My father worked for an insurance company in the city of Liverpool. Life was quite routine and straightforward in our household. I was growing up in the post-war era of the 1950/60's, and like most people of that time, our lives seemed settled for the long haul in the immediate local community.

Our mothers stayed at home as housewives and our fathers went out to work. Most people stayed in the same house all their life and most men stayed with the same job or company all of their working life. Looking back, I am extremely grateful for the stability and security I received from this routine and safe way of life.

Black and white television was something only a very few people owned and if they did, the programs were extremely limited. Car owners were also few and far between in the fifties which meant there was great reliance on public transport and it was not unusual to walk long distances to shops and services. To travel fifty miles was considered a long journey and usually this kind of travel only happened when you went on holiday. To go overseas was hardly ever heard of unless someone was emigrating. Attending a local church was part of ordinary British life at that time and most of my friends went to one Sunday school or another.

My family attended an evangelical Presbyterian church, which meant traveling a fair distance and as my father was a deacon and Sunday school superintendent we did this journey three times each Sunday! Until I was twelve years old, we took the bus to church and this entailed a walk of twenty minutes to the no. 85 bus stop which in turn took us the two and a half miles to our destination. The no. 80 bus, which would have spared us the twenty minute walk, didn't run on Sundays.

For me, if I chose not to go to church in the evening on Sunday it usually meant the time was spent at home with my mother singing from the *Golden Bells Hymn Book* or *Redemption Hymnal*. My strict Christian upbringing didn't allow me to play with my friends in the road on Sunday or go to watch my friend's television, which of course was by far my preferred option.

Because I grew up without the entertainment facilities we have today, it meant an environment was created where I was thrilled and excited when we had visitors to our house or went to a meeting where a guest was speaking. I clearly remember being inspired by stories from missionaries who stayed in our home. They often spoke of how God had answered their prayers.

My mother would also tell me stories of missionaries whom God had used in exciting ways. These missionaries were heroes of our faith in my mind. Hence, when they came to stay at our house, I would sit and listen to all they had to say. Looking back, I know that seeds of faith were being planted deep in my heart. I can't remember a time when I doubted that God was able to act in any given situation or doubted that He heard and answered prayer.

My parents held prayer meetings in our home for various mission organizations and they attended many prayer meetings. My mother was a prayerful lady and became a member of the Lydia Fellowship (a women's national prayer network) and led her own group. In my adult Christian years, I was never particularly attracted to prayer meetings. I preferred what I saw as 'action' and involved myself in Sunday school teaching, door to door evangelistic work or in various church projects. Somehow, I always saw prayer meetings as being too static or boring! However, prayer for me was fundamental to my actions and I was inspired by the times that prayers were answered during the action. I had a kind of 'pray as you go' attitude to life.

It's often in retrospect, that we can see how God has worked in our lives and it's in looking back that we can make sense of the present. For me this is so true. Living life as a very normal person from an ordinary background, I didn't realize that some of the experiences I had in life were in fact God's way of preparing me for the future and also speaking to me of His nature and His ways.

It's only now that I can fully appreciate and put into words the significance of certain events (like the lady in the toilet). God was clearly using such events to make me trust Him and learn more of Him in my life. As a result I would be able to see His kingdom come here on earth, and His love reaching out.

It's from this perspective that I write on intercession. In my experience intercession has been intensely practical. For me, it has been something I have been part of and seen outworked in the practicalities of daily living. I write on the healing aspect, because God called me to the healing ministry, so that's where my experience of God moving in extraordinary and wonderful ways comes from. However the principles remain the same for other situations and circumstances which aren't related to healing but are the outworking of our Christian lives.

A growing desire to help others

Both my brother and my sister were high achievers academically. I, on the other hand, didn't fulfill my parents' expectations in this regard! I mentioned earlier in the chapter that it's sometimes only in retrospect that we can see God's plan and purposes in our lives. So it was with me.

In my growing years I had a natural desire to help people who were less fortunate than me. Even as a small child I can remember bringing home friends who had problems, whether it be a grazed knee or that I deemed them in need of some cakes and drink. At school I was often reprimanded for not concentrating and this would usually be because I was trying to help someone else rather than doing my own work.

All in all, I was very much a 'people person' and this was my motivation in life. For whatever reason, qualifications or academic knowledge never gripped me. My mother thought I would make a nurse and I was encouraged in this direction. However, I would never have made it as a nurse because I hated blood and gore, injections and the like! The thought of attending operations appalled me.

In the absence of any real career path, I decided office work would do for me and I joined a two year secretarial course. From there I managed to find what was then considered to be a quite highly paid job in the city of Liverpool. Life was running its course. It was during my years at secretarial college that I left our Presbyterian church and joined a very lively and popular Anglican church. Many of my friends attended this particular Anglican Church as it had an excellent youth group. For me, it meant moving away from my parents' influence, which was a typical teenage thing to do. I went with their blessing.

It was at St. Mary's that I began to grow and develop my Christian life in a new way. I was encouraged to use my gifts and skills and it was here I felt spiritually at home. There was an outward looking youth group and a program of events which brought me in touch with many people from all walks of life. I was happily fulfilled in living my life.

Marriage and children kept me busy alongside part time work and my life seemed settled. The years passed, and then everything which had seemed normal suddenly wasn't. Nothing can prepare you for the trauma of divorce and I faced deep shock and pain arising from my first husband's unfaithfulness and our subsequent marriage breakdown. It took many years for me to recover and to discern the plans the Lord had for me.

For most of my life, I had been engaged in many kinds of Christian activities through the various Anglican churches I attended. Looking back now, I can see God was using this time to prepare me for something He had for me in the future, in particular the healing ministry.

I was involved with our church in local evangelism, which in those days meant that we visited houses or blocks of flats in the city and invited people to come to the forthcoming gospel service. Invariably, I would end up in conversations and situations in which the people I visited would pour out their problems in life.

I came from a protected and sheltered background and some of these problems were beyond anything I had even heard of, let alone could help with. Yet, something in me was filled with compassion and a desire to help. Whether it was people with depression, physical sickness, alcoholism in the family, suicidal feelings or people in need of someone to care, something inside me told me there were answers. I was frustrated that inviting them to Church didn't seem to be enough. There had to be more for them.

I knew the people needed to hear about Jesus and come to know Him. But I thought, somehow, they needed a *bridge*. They needed to have their needs met. They needed to know that the God we were bringing to them had real and practical answers for their problems. I would feel incredibly inadequate in saying anything, let alone in trying to do anything. I had all this faith inside me but I had no idea how to apply it in these situations.

John Wimber's visit

It was in the midst of these dilemmas that I learned, through my church, of an American pastor by the name of John Wimber. John Wimber had apparently written a book about evangelism with signs and wonders. This was it! This was what was needed! I hoped this would be the answer to our prayers. I could hardly contain my excitement when my vicar invited me to join him, his wife and one other church member at an open meeting in a local Baptist church, where John Wimber would be speaking on evangelism with signs and wonders.

I attended this meeting with no pre-conceived ideas or expectations. In fact, I was quite nervous and fearful. Although I had experienced the baptism in the Holy Spirit during the 1970's charismatic renewal, I was never the kind of person to act in an irrational way and was naturally quite cautious. John Wimber spoke to the congregation before there was any prayer or worship. I thought he was giving some announcements, the usual Christian thing to do before a meeting begins. Instead he quietly and simply said that he was going to ask the Lord to visit us and would we please get ready.

I had never heard language like this and didn't know what to make of it, so I turned to the lady next to me and whispered, "Do you know what he means?" She seemed as puzzled as myself and replied, "oh just hold your hands up and see what happens!" With my eyes tightly shut I obeyed. In the silence which followed, I was completely taken aback by what I can only describe as the brightest sense of the presence of Jesus and a peace which was overwhelming. I thought everyone was experiencing the same thing and so I remained standing while a prayer team came around the room.

I don't know who or how many of this team prayed for me, but it didn't last long. The abiding words which penetrated my heart were those words which spoke of me being used by God to bring healing to others. Without doubt, this was a time God used to draw me more fully into His purposes. Something was affirmed and strengthened in my inner being by the Spirit of God for a destiny to come.

Sadly, our vicar was not impressed by John Wimber and I can't remember to this day what the rest of the evening was about. I had received an encounter with God and this was an incredibly precious experience which transcended anything else which took place that evening. We all went home in silence. I can remember the next day in church being introduced to a lady who had just broken her arm. Our vicar bluntly told her that I believed I had a healing ministry! In that moment, I felt so helpless and embarrassed. I prayed the only prayer I knew how to pray at the time, "Oh God please heal this lady's arm!" My faith was buried underneath my embarrassment and my desire to run away home as soon as possible.

Our church was a big church and I never inquired or found out anything about the lady's arm but I felt certain that no healing took place. Inner questions bombarded me. Who was I to think God could use me? I was just an ordinary person with no anointing whatsoever and I should leave these holier things to those who had the gifts and who were ordained or much more special than I was. Again, in retrospect, the enemy was having a field day with my mind and emotions. What a complete and utter fool I was to even think that God was calling me. I took refuge in the routine of my day to day life, bringing up my children.

A new healing ministry

I was involved in our house group, Sunday school work, flower arranging at church and various outreaches in my local area. Yet, I knew there was more. The days of inviting people to go to a local crusade were long gone and even our local coffee morning outreach was mostly serving Christians. There was a spiritual frustration which didn't die away and it longed to be satisfied. It was around this time that news came to our area of a vision for a healing ministry. As I read the leaflet, everything inside me jumped. I knew this was for me and I enrolled to attend the prayer support meetings which were being held to pray for the fulfillment of the vision.

This vision came into fruition (and is now internationally known as Ellel Ministries). A center for the healing ministry was to be acquired near junction 33 of the M6 motorway. Peter Horrobin, the visionary founder, was recruiting team members to pray for people in need. I knew this was something God wanted me to do and in trepidation I signed up. Little did I know then that I would eventually marry Peter and God's redemptive purposes would be worked out in both our lives in extraordinary ways.

During the six month period between signing the initial contract and the actual completion of the purchase of Ellel Grange, various healing services were held in churches throughout the north of England. Many local churches had given finance towards the vision.

It was on one such occasion that the team took a healing service in a large Anglican church in Lancashire. I was about to receive one of my first lessons about intercessory prayer. The church was filled to capacity and Peter spoke powerfully about God's desire to heal. At the end he invited those who would like prayer to come forward. A long line of people straddling the whole length of the church emerged! Along with others, I was urged to come to the front and pray with these folk.

I stood at the front of the line filled with a mixture of spiritual anticipation and excitement, yet struggling with my own inadequacy and fears. My natural instinct was to hide away. I had never been one for standing in front of a crowd, whether at school, at college, at church or anywhere else. 'The less people noticed me the better' was part of my make up. God has had to do a deep work in me to release me from overwhelming timidity and fear.

As I watched the line of people grow, my eyes alighted on a lady whose arm was in a sling. My human nature said, "I hope she doesn't come to me" because I imagined she wouldn't be healed and then what would everybody think of this new healing ministry? They wouldn't see it as being powerful at all. My memory went back to the day in church where I had prayed for the lady with a broken arm. All my emotions followed suit and in those few moments my whole body was shaking with fear. Here was I, someone who thought they had faith and who dared to believe God had called me and could use me in bringing healing to others and I was shaking from top to bottom!

My worst fears were realized as this lady approached me for prayer. She was smaller than I was and I had to bend down to hear what she was saying. I summoned up my very best opening line and asked, "What would you like me to pray for?" It was hardly profound and as I braced myself to pray in faith for healing of her arm, she took me completely by surprise by replying in her broad north-country English accent, *"I've bin ealed luv, take them bandages off!"*

It took a while for what she had said to sink in ("I've been healed"), and I found myself replying, "are you sure?" Here I was, supposed to be full of faith, and I was not exactly adding to her faith! With exasperation, she replied, *"of course I'm sure, get them bandages off!"*

By now my natural mind was being filled with the worst possible scenario. This is a new healing ministry. If I take her bandages off and she isn't healed, then all the newspapers will be filled with stories like, *'New Healing Ministry Goes Against Doctors Orders.'* Doubts and fears flooded my mind and my inner being, obliterating any measure of faith I thought I had mustered up.

I quickly determined that I should go and ask Peter what to do. He was busy praying for someone else and in the spur of the moment he told me to take her behind some pews and quietly assess her arm – such was his faith! By this time the lady herself was attempting to remove the bandages and her husband was wagging his finger and shouting at her, "you know them doctors told you not to take them bandages off for six weeks!" I, on the other hand was expecting her to have a gush of pain at any moment and she, in the absence of any pain, kept telling me, "I've bin ealed." Well, God has a sense of humor and, to my amazement, this lady went down the aisle of the church waving her arm and telling people of her healing.

God was confirming His commissioning on this new ministry. The lady had sat and listened to the message, her heart had responded and God answered her as she sat in the pew. The Lord taught me a critical lesson through this experience. I had thought I had to do it. I had taken the responsibility as mine. Would I have the right words to say, the right prayers to pray? And what if she wasn't healed?

God taught me that day, right at the outset of my journey in the healing ministry that this was not about me but all about Him. It was about His power to heal and what He is able to do. All He's looking for is willing, obedient hearts. He's looking for those who, even in their weakness and human-ness, are willing to be available to Him as channels of His love, mercy and grace. It's in this relationship between the human and the divine that God works out His purposes. It's very releasing for us to realize that we are simply the vessel, the clay pot!

I would love to be able to write that from there on, the healing ministry was simple and that God just 'did it' without any effort on my part in every situation. However, because there is our humanity and fallen nature too, there were many lessons to learn. Now twenty years later, after interceding for hundreds of individuals, I feel privileged to be able to share some of the keys the Lord has given and revealed in His love.

Intercession and healing go hand in hand – they are inseparable. If I have learnt anything at all from the years of pioneering and battling in the healing ministry, it's that healing in its simplicity is bringing the heart of God to the heart of man. Intercession is the relationship between a Holy God and sinful man - how God can use an earthen vessel to fulfill His purposes! It never ceases to amaze me that a Holy God desires and looks for a person who wants to walk with Him and know Him for who He really is.

I have long since found out that the only way any of us can experience healing and peace within is by seeking God for who He is. He's our creator and He knows each of us individually, far more than we ever know ourselves.

Healing takes place in an individual life when, in the inner being, a connection is made to *Truth*. I am expressing the word 'Truth' here with a capital 'T' because it's through Jesus that we have the Truth. He's the Truth and it's His Truth that sets us free. Only He knows the depth of what's in our hearts. As human beings we look on the outward appearance (even of our own hearts) and we need Jesus and His Holy Spirit to lead and direct us in His *Truth*.

When the doors of Ellel Grange were opened, there was a constant stream of people seeking help for their problems. These problems ranged from marriage issues, addictions, obsessions, mental illness, physical illness, occult bondage, sexual bondages and depression to the worst kind of abuses and man's inhumanity to man. Unimaginable stories unfolded as people unburdened themselves to the new and inexperienced team.

I certainly had a heart for people and a desire to see God move in each life, but I knew I was totally incapable and inadequate for the situations we were facing. My home life and background of inner security proved to be invaluable during times of intense struggle and battling to win through. I knew I had to pray. And pray I did! I didn't know *how* or *what* to pray. I didn't hold prayer meetings, but I knew to cry out to God in my heart, and sometimes out loud, for all I was worth.

It's out of the countless hopeless and intransigent situations we found ourselves in, that I write this book. In the intercessory struggle and through times of weeping and crying out to God for help, we found He *is* faithful. We discovered many keys of the kingdom and how to overcome the enemy of souls with the weapon of truth and in the power of God's love and might. It's out of this crucible of intercession that this book has emerged, bringing valuable keys for the healing ministry.

I pray that some of our journey and experience will be a benefit and blessing to you, if you're looking for keys and answers in your own life. May God bless you in your walk with Him.

The Intercessory Place

It was a typical late winter's day in England. Outside the Ellel Grange center a gale was blowing, rain was pouring down and it was cold. No-one would have wanted to go outside in this weather and I certainly didn't. However, the dog needed a walk to do what dogs do! I donned my coat and warm woollies and braced myself for the walk around the perimeter of what we call 'the circle' which is a pathway surrounded by fields near the center. At that time of year it's not unusual to see the first lambs in the field.

As I passed by the large fields, I became aware of a small grey bundle at the foot of a large old oak tree with a knobbly and gnarled trunk. It was a tiny newborn lamb and I thought it was dead. I looked about to see where the mother sheep were, but there were none around. The little lamb had been abandoned. Without thinking any further I tied the dog to a post and climbed over the iron railing fence and then a barbed wire fence and picked up the soggy, wet and cold little lamb. As I placed him inside my coat, the faintest bleat greeted me.

Hearing the little lamb's faint bleat spurred me on to reach help. I realized he was dying. At the bottom of the Ellel Grange drive-way lies a farmhouse with a Christian farmer and although the lamb had not been found in his fields, I knew he would care for the lamb. I knocked on the farmhouse door with urgency and when Alec opened it, a sense of relief flooded through me. He took one look at the little lamb, held his big rugged hand out towards it and gave me a big smile, "don't worry", he said. "I will put him by the fire and give him a nice warm bottle and he will soon be strong again and back in the fields with his brothers and sisters".

My mission accomplished, I left the farm filled with elation. I had rescued a lamb from sure death. What a joy! It was at this precise moment that the Spirit of God spoke to me. Into my spirit came these words, "there are many of my lambs in the fields, lost and abandoned, bleeding and dying with no-one to rescue them. Will you find them and bring them to me?" My heart was still so full at having rescued the lamb that I found myself replying, "Yes Lord, I will help them." Tears began to run down my cheeks as I was profoundly touched by the presence of the Lord.

It was then that I looked down at my coat and saw that it was torn from the barbed wire and that my clothes were muddy and dirty. The Spirit of the Lord spoke to me again saying, "This work is costly. It cost My Son everything to rescue His lambs. Are you willing to pay the price?" In my tears, I found myself saying from the depth of my being, "yes Lord, I am willing, please help me."

Thus began a journey for me, and also the Ellel team, of watching the Father heart of God bring restoration and food to many lives in need of rescue or shelter from the harsh elements of life and from enemy attack, so that they could be fed and made strong again for their life destiny. It's a precious privilege to bring His lambs to Him for healing and restoration. The cost has been outweighed by the joy and reward of experiencing the abundant life Jesus came to bring in the lives of so many who were shattered and broken. The Lord was teaching me about intercession.

Whenever we engage in prayer on behalf of another, or indeed on behalf of ourselves, we enter the intercessory place. We are seeking God's face for a situation to change or something to come into being which has hitherto not happened. We are asking God to intervene somehow. We may not think in terms of us being part of the answer. We would be more likely to assume that our praying is the work we need to do. In one sense it *is* the work we need to do, because it's through prayer that we communicate.

However God is looking for more than simply the words and there are many aspects to prayer which are more than words. Even so, at a later stage in the book, we *will* look at words, because words in themselves are a powerful tool in our armory. However, God is looking for us to be part of the answer and to apply some of the principles He has given us, in order to work with Him in bringing about the kingdom of God here on earth.

To help us really enter the intercessory place effectively, we may need to dispense with a few blind spots or mindsets, for example viewing prayer like a quiver full of arrows, some of which may hit the target and others may not. From this perspective, prayer can become a way of telling God about the problem and even going so far as to tell Him how to resolve it!

On the other hand we may have developed an 'if it be Thy will' approach to prayer, leaving the only possible solution to God. However, this is a rather detached way of praying, a kind of hit or miss affair where we're left wondering whether God has heard us or not. The true intercessory place is where our whole being is engaged in prayer and in fact God may want to use us as part of the answer to our prayers.

In the Lord Jesus Christ we have our model intercessor. The gospel of John in chapter seventeen, describes the role of intercession through the prayer of Jesus to His Father in heaven. Jesus interceded on behalf of those He loved. He became their representative to God the Father and His prayers were powerful and certain because Jesus was part of the answer. He had walked the walk, He had fought the fight, and He was willing to pay the price.

It was because of the Lord Jesus' willingness and obedience to His Father that He was able to access the Father's will and know it so clearly. He and His Father are one and together with the Holy Spirit they form a loving triune relationship of purpose. Their harmonious serving of one another fulfills the greatest purpose of the Godhead which is to bring mankind back into the Father's love and protection and to give them His inheritance.

So it's here that we have practical clues to intercession and answered prayer. Perhaps the most important question is are we

willing to be part of the answer? And secondly, does that willingness translate into obedience? Sometimes the old saying, "the spirit
is willing but the flesh is weak" can be relevant because of our
own humanity and weaknesses. I personally feel that there are vast
numbers of unanswered prayers because God needs us to be part
of that answer and a lot of the time we have been afraid or we
didn't know how to participate in the answer.

It's a mystery, but God has ordained that humankind be submitted to Him in caring for the earth we live in. It's in relationship with Him that His purposes are brought about. Jesus prayed a
model prayer for us to follow when He said, *"our Father in heaven,
hallowed be your name, your kingdom come on earth as it is in heaven"*.
He then went on to say, *"forgive us our sins as we forgive the sins of
others."* This gives us the clue that somehow our heart's condition
and attitude has something to do with the answer to prayer.

Of course a sovereign, almighty God can do anything by Himself.
One truth is that God can do anything without us. However, this
can be used as an excuse for abdicating our God-given responsibility. The opposite and equal truth is that God has chosen to limit
Himself to relationship with humankind. There may be times
when God does work in a sovereign way without any human inter-
ference but Scripture is clear that God looks at man's choices and
obedience and His purposes are carried out through these choices
and obedience.

In the New Testament, we see how God's purpose was to work
in and through people in relationship with them. Jesus gave the
disciples the Holy Spirit to be His presence and comfort with
them. He also gave them the power of His Holy Spirit to exercise
kingdom authority. He told them to go out in His name and do the
work of the kingdom and He would be with them even to the end
of the age (Matthew 28:20).

We see in 2 Corinthians 4:7 that it is God's plan and desire to
use us as vessels or channels of His love, grace and mercy. Having
received the love of God for ourselves, we would in turn pour
this out to others. Jesus, our intercessor, prayed for us before His
Father that we would have love one for another (John 13:35).

God's love is a multifaceted diamond but there can be no love at all without action. In looking at intercession, which is the very heart of God Himself, above all we see love in action. How does God express His heart of love through us and how does this change the spiritual climate and in turn change an attitude, change a belief, change a person, change a situation?

God's not waiting for us to be perfect individuals, nor somehow to be angels! If He had wanted us to be angels, He would have made us that way! He created us human beings with the gift of free will. God didn't design us as robots or automatons. He risked giving us the gift of free will because without us having this freedom there could be no authentic relationship. The freedom to say yes or no is an extremely precious part of relationship and a gift given by our loving creator God.

It's incredibly releasing to know that God already knows our fallibility and yes, our incapacity to attain to His standard. The greatest gift of all that God gave us was when through His Son Jesus, we received His righteousness. God, our heavenly Father hears our prayers and our lives given to Him because we are seen as righteous and acceptable. When Jesus freely gave Himself up to death on our behalf, He covered our sinfulness.

Our Heavenly Father loves us and He embraces us in a heart full of love. Our relationship with Him is restored and He can now open the floodgates of heaven and pour upon us our inheritance. The whole story of the prodigal son shows us just how much our Father loves us. He simply wants our hearts to turn to Him, to trust Him, to allow Him to be Father and for us to enter into being a child of His kingdom.

It's an amazing fact that we don't have to beg God to answer our prayers. In fact Scripture tells us that He already knows and answers before we call (Isaiah 65:24) and while we are speaking He will hear.

Sometimes our fallen and flawed humanity can't comprehend, discern or receive the way God is answering. For this reason, the intercessory place is of the highest importance and value in our Christian walk. I have learnt (and am still learning!) that the ways of God are not the ways of man (me)! (Isaiah 55:8). One thing we can be absolutely sure of is that not one of our thoughts, needs, cries, insecurities, demands, bewilderments and confusions will ever go unheard. Neither will they ever be disregarded or discarded. Matthew 10:30 tells us, *"even the very hairs on your head are counted."*

Child-like trust

A small child has a very transient perspective on life compared to his adult father. The small child is in his world of today, playing with a favorite toy, demanding a sweetie – now! For this small child the world is now and his needs are now – there's no awareness of a greater picture, of a greater goal or a greater good. He can't comprehend that at some time in the future whatever his father is doing today will be his legacy, his inheritance and for his greater good. It would be futile for the child to cause his father to leave the greater picture to attend to all his son's wants for today, rather than have a bigger picture of his son's needs for the future.

One of the most important lessons I have learnt in my own walk with the Lord and in helping others with theirs is that our wants are not always what we need and our needs are not always what we want. Like very small children with a loving, mature, caring, providing Father – we must come to God our Heavenly Father in childlike trust. Sometimes, we may cry, kick or scream because it seems life is not going our way. Sometimes, we may be in the deepest pain and suffering. Sometimes, we may desire or want something so badly and we want it now. Sometimes, we long to see another helped, set free, healed or become a Christian. Sometimes we need a solution to a big problem or an answer to a decision which needs to be made.

Whatever our relationship with God is like, we all need to learn more deeply that we are children and He is our Father. There are some things we can understand and learn and others are part of a bigger purpose and plan we can't yet see, and what He requires of us is trust. Trust is the highest form of relationship. I have seen how hard many people in need of healing find it to trust anyone. Their trust in God is fragile and because of this they're constantly looking for outward signs of His presence rather than having peace in the depth of their being. When we come to God as children with an all-sufficient, totally dependable Heavenly Father, this is the place where God hears and answers prayer. Later in the book we will look at how out of mistrust, 'soulish' praying can take over that place, and the enemy can intrude.

The intercessory place is when we come to our God out of our relationship with Him and place our hearts in His. It's also when we receive His heart into ours. Ever since God the Father sent a part of Himself, His precious Son Jesus, to dwell with us mortal beings, the way was opened up for us to be in relationship with God.

When the Lord Jesus was born, He brought the greatest gift of all to humankind. He scrolled back the skies and revealed eternity. Life was no longer transient for us. Jesus (our great intercessor) made the way for life to be eternal! How incredible that Jesus through His coming, His death and His resurrection made the way for us to enter the eternal and to participate with the Godhead - Father, Son and Holy Spirit in His plans and purposes.

This is the intercessory place. It's a trusting relationship between human beings and God. God our Father created us for relationship. He made us in His image. The bible in Genesis 1:31 says that when God was speaking about what He made, He said, *"it is good!"* Our Heavenly Father desires that we participate with Him in building His kingdom. His kingdom is our kingdom; He's building it for us to inherit with Him! The Scripture tells us we are 'co-heirs with Christ' (Ephesians 3:6).

In a loving relationship with Him, we can join with Him in the bigger picture, even though we don't understand it fully – yet! Just as the small child in his home with his adult father can't fully comprehend why 'daddy' is building an extension or earning money (for the child's education) or why he's careful to guard valuable possessions, so it is that we often don't comprehend why our Father has another agenda other than our immediate often self-focused one.

A loving earthly father will teach and correct a child so that the child learns good things – safety, manners, kindness to others, knowledge. These good things are to help the child to grow. Many times these lessons are not received as good, but they are for the child's ultimate good. An uncaring parent will ignore the child and allow it to find its own way with an immature and distorted perspective of life and people.

As children of a loving Heavenly Father who holds a wealth of understanding, wisdom and treasure that He longs for us to participate in, we are designed to learn from Him the safety, the protocol and the keys of His kingdom in order that we can become all that He wants us to be and in turn we can participate fully with Him in seeing heaven released on earth and His kingdom built, which will eventually be our inheritance.

Just as a small child learns from their father's actions, behavior or attitude and from seeing his heart towards others, so we, as children of our Heavenly Father, learn from Him. We watch as He does things, we imitate Him, and then we grow into His likeness. He has so *much* to teach us and so *much* to give us – much more than we can think or imagine. Perhaps this book can help us to come afresh as small children to our wonderful Heavenly Father, to participate with Him in learning and growing. We'll experience pain sometimes but also the joys and blessings of belonging to Him.

The Intercessory Mandate

Is not this the fast that I choose; to loose the bonds of injustice, to undo the thongs of the yoke, to let the oppressed go free, and to break every yoke?

Is it not to share your bread with the hungry, and bring the homeless poor into your house; when you see the naked to cover them and not to hide yourself from your own kin?

Then your light shall break forth like the dawn, and your healing shall spring up quickly; your vindicator shall go before you, the glory of the Lord shall be your rear guard.

Then you shall call, and the Lord will answer; you shall cry for help, and he will say, here I am.

If you remove the yoke from among you, the pointing of the finger, the speaking of evil, if you offer your food to the hungry and satisfy the needs of the afflicted, then your light shall rise in the darkness and your gloom be like the noonday.

The Lord will guide you continually, and satisfy your needs in parched places, and make your bones strong; and you shall be like a watered garden, like a spring of water, whose waters never fail.

Your ancient ruins shall be rebuilt; you shall raise up the foundations of many generations; you shall be called the repairer of the breach, the restorer of streets to live in."

Isaiah 58:6-12

Isaiah is describing true worship and speaking out the prophetic voice and passion of God. These words reveal to us the heart of God and are the keys for His power, presence and life to be out-poured upon us and for the redemption and re-building of so much which has been ruined and is in need of restoration.

Sometime we think of fasting as simply sacrificing food. This passage in Isaiah tells us otherwise. There is also another kind of fasting which God requires. In verse six the requirement is to loose the bonds of injustice and to undo the thongs of the yoke and to let the oppressed go free. Whenever you minister healing and deliverance to people in Jesus' name, you're undoing the bonds of injustice.

In setting people free spiritually, we are fulfilling a scriptural mandate. It's an intercessory role, in that we are standing in the gap on behalf of someone else and we are applying the keys of the kingdom so they can receive release from oppression.

I have often felt at the end of my tether in ministry situations. Listening to someone's deep emotional pain and problems can be draining. Pouring strength, love and hope into a person's empty heart is not always easy. Giving of yourself when you feel there's nothing left (even when God is strengthening you) can be a great struggle. It's in these situations that we find the heart of God truly responds to our giving of ourselves on behalf of another and our obedience to His ways. It's through our sacrificial honoring of His desires that He responds by releasing His promises and anointing for healing and restoration.

Spiritually speaking we are sharing our bread (verse seven) with the hungry and bringing the homeless poor into our house (heart) and covering the naked (giving spiritual protection). Our Father who knows all things is watching as we share what we have, the food of life with those who are spiritually hungry and who're in need of a spiritual home in order to be protected (covered) for a time until they regain strength and healing. His promises are sure and swift (verse eight). Our light shall break forth like the dawn and our healing will spring up quickly.

There's a principle here in the intercessory mandate when we pray for healing for others. Our own healing will be accelerated through our willingness to give to others and our obedience to God's principles. It doesn't end here because the words in Isaiah go on to say that our vindicator (God Himself) will go before us and His glory will be our rear guard (verses eight and nine). In essence God gives His promise to us that, if we fulfill His plans and purposes in places where we are misunderstood, misjudged, misrepresented or betrayed, God's own glory will be our rear guard. What can this possibly mean?

From experience, I'm left in no doubt that God vindicates His Holy purposes. When the Lord sees the heart, the sacrifice, and the willingness of His people to participate in His Holy purposes, He will vindicate them. This doesn't mean that mistakes are never made. But (praise God!) we have a God who doesn't judge the outer appearance but who looks upon the heart and is able to judge it.

God will bring a vindication and His glory will be seen when we give of ourselves on behalf of another with a right motive and when it costs us something. When we want God's purposes rather than seeking to have our own needs met, not doing things to make ourselves feel good, look good or to control others God will bring forth fruit and all the fruit will belong to Him. But God will do it in His way and in His time. This will be despite our inadequacy.

Within the work of Ellel Ministries for example, many people have paid a price to bring God's heart to others and as a result there's an anointing on the ministry which has seen countless thousands come to transformation, restoration and healing. This is God's fruit, it belongs to Him, and it is for His glory.

When the glory of God is seen and experienced, it brings with it a rear guard of protection (outlined in this passage in Isaiah) which vindicates those who have placed their trust and hope in Him. Truly, if we call upon the Lord, He will answer! Our God is more willing to help than we are to call and verse nine of Isaiah 58 is an extremely precious promise for us to hold on to, *"you shall cry for help, and he will say, here I am"*.

There are many 'ifs' in the bible yet this one in Isaiah 58:9-12 is extremely profound and relevant to intercession and healing.

The Lord is requiring us (on the same level as abstinence or fasting) to remove the pointing finger and the speaking of evil. As I have pondered this in my own life and in helping others come to healing, I have seen countless times how we as carnal, fallen, fallible individuals take up the place of judge of others and go on to speak evil of them.

If ever there was a barrier to healing and restoration this is it. Satan wants the place of judge, a place only God Himself can have, but we know Satan is the usurper of God, the one who would be as God. Yet, we too, like to judge. We judge ourselves, we judge others and we judge God. It is a sobering thought that we're giving power to the enemy by taking up God's place as judge and agreeing with Satan! There's a right weighing and testing which is a righteous judging of issues, but in both the Old and the New Testament we are strongly warned about the tongue and about condemning others.

There is a law of sowing and reaping which comes into operation and if we sow in the flesh then we will reap in the flesh, with all manner of consequences, including health issues. However if we sow in the spirit, in God's love and grace, we will reap righteous consequences.

The 'if' of Isaiah 58, tells us that if we fulfill the conditions of giving ourselves on behalf of those in need and we do away with the carnal issues of judging and the speaking of evil we will reap wonderful benefits. For we as human beings weren't made divine with the capacity to judge like our all- knowing, fair and just Heavenly Father. Satisfying the needs of the afflicted will cause light to rise in your darkness (verse 10) and even your gloom to be as noonday! The Lord will guide you continually and satisfy your needs when you are parched and He will make your bones strong (verse 11).

In the next part of this chapter in Isaiah, God is describing to us His most faithful promise. If we can only grasp this and enter into His heart for the oppressed, He will make us, as the Body of Christ together, into a well-watered garden, like a spring of water whose waters never fail (verse 11). We will always be those who have life to give to others.

Incredibly, God also promises that our ancient ruins will be rebuilt. I often wondered what our ancient ruins were and I have now come to realize that these ruins are those things in need of restoration in *our* lives, whether they come to us from our generational history or whether they in our own lifetime. God wants to restore the consequences of our painful and difficult past. He wants to break the inherited generational curses of such things as alcoholism, addictions, health problems, and abuse.

The intercessory mandate is here for us to see in verse twelve. If we can grasp and enter into the fast which God requires and stand in the gap on behalf of another or to put it simply, to be the arms, the feet, the voice, the heart of Jesus for another for whom we are praying, we will see God move in power in order that they can receive His life and restoration. We will be known as those who *'repair the breach and the restorer of streets to live in'.*

The heart of God

Seeing people healed is all about this act of intercession. At the foundation of all the wonderful keys God gives us for healing, must be the heart of God Himself. It's so easy to act out of technique or experience, but we should never forget that it's the willingness and obedience to be sacrificially giving of ourselves on behalf of another, for the right motives, which God anoints and uses powerfully.

I was once asked to do a talk on "what is healing?" Perhaps people thought I would come out with some profound keys and insights from my years of experience but as I prepared, I found myself answering with the simplest of answers. "Healing is Jesus and Jesus is healing". Healing is all to do with relationship with Jesus no matter what our condition is. Our job as those who seek healing for others is primarily an intercessory role. It's bringing Jesus in all His truth, His grace and His love to people's lives so that they can enter into their Heavenly Father's inheritance.

There's a sobering passage of Scripture in the New Testament which once again brings the heart of God to the heart of man. Jesus is talking to His followers about the time when He will come again and sit on His throne of glory to judge the nations.

Let's look at one of the most challenging passages in the whole bible where Jesus is speaking to His followers about the separation of the sheep and the goats.

"Truly I tell you, just as you did it to one of the least of these who are members of my family, you did it to me. Then He will say to those at his left hand, 'You that are accursed, depart from me into the eternal fire prepared for the devil and his angels; for I was hungry and you gave me no food, I was thirsty and you gave me nothing to drink. I was a stranger and you did not welcome me, naked and you did not give me clothing, sick and in prison and you did not visit me.' Then they will also answer, 'Lord, when was it that we saw you hungry or thirsty or a stranger or naked or sick or in prison, and did not take care of you?' Then he will answer them, 'truly I tell you, just as you did not do it to one of the least of these, you did not do it to me.' And these will go away into eternal punishment but the righteous into eternal life."

Matthew 25:37-46

Here we see the intercessory heart of God. Jesus is showing us that outside of relationship, there's nothing. His model for intercession is participation, He calls us to be part of the answer and for all we do to be motivated out of our love relationship with Him. If we're not motivated by His love and His compassion for others, then in effect, we have no relationship with God either. Jesus said, *"If you love me, you will obey me."* He's not looking for our grudging or patronizing help. Jesus desires a relationship of joy, a pure love which in the natural realm we love to see reflected between a parent and a child.

We know God and He knows us, not through our 'works of performance' but through our love and service expressed in the intercessory role of serving and loving others as unto Him.

Principles for Seeing the Power of God Flow in Healing

Divine multiplication in team work

God the Father, God the Son and God the Holy Spirit are a team! They work together as one in relational harmony to bring about the plans and purposes of the whole.

When God made man, He made us in His image. He made us relational beings with a body, soul and spirit (1 Thessalonians 5:23), each of these three parts designed to relate together with their own specific function and purpose in unity for the good of the whole person. God saw that it wasn't good for man to live alone (Genesis 2:18) and He provided a helper and companion in woman and He designed procreation for the purpose of setting people in family. This was the Father's plan for us to have a home, a place to belong and security. This in turn would prepare the way for our spiritual home with Him in eternity (John 14:2).

Jesus in His coming to earth demonstrated family and team-work. There were times when He needed to be alone with His Heavenly Father but He placed Himself among those He knew and loved as family, and among those people with whom He carried out His Father's plans. There's a right place for solitude and for being alone with God and it's true that for some, geographical or physical situations make it impossible to be with others. However, we see from Scripture that Jesus sent His disciples out in twos and it's not God's design for us to work completely independently or in isolation.

Team work is part of God's intercessory plan to bring about His purposes. When we receive Jesus into our lives, we become His child. All of us as His children are part of His family. In the healing ministry many people come for help because they have never experienced family and belonging, or they have had God's plan for family distorted and even shattered.

It's a great privilege to be an intercessory *bridge* in bringing people to the heart of God and into His truth for belonging and family. In this fallen world there are no ideals but nevertheless, the heart of the Father yearns for His children to know Him in the core of who they are, so in all of life's outward circumstances they can know protection, safety and peace. This in essence is true healing. The family of God was designed by Him to be a team working together in unity for one purpose, modeling who He is as Father.

In this place of joint purpose we will experience God's anointing and blessing. God is not looking for a *guru* individual who holds all the gifting and anointing. He knows that no single human person has this capability or they would be God!

God's looking for those who are willing to work together with Him and with each other, to carry out His will. God's looking for a team! The Apostle Paul describes the family of God here on earth as the body of Christ (1 Corinthians 12:27).

We are joined to Him as the head and to each other as a necessary and valuable part of the whole. Can the foot say to the eye, *"I do not need you"*? Each part of the body is vital if it is to work as it's intended to do, as a reflection of who our Heavenly Father is. In fact, Paul explains in Ephesians 4:16 that when each separate part works as it should, *'the whole body grows and builds itself up in love'*.

Team work provides the environment where love is expressed and demonstrated. When we have been praying for people with deeply broken lives who have never known a true model of love, we have seen transformation in them and healing of their inner needs and wounds through experiencing love in the team. They experienced the team giving love to them and to each other. Over the years we have lost count of how many times people have approached us to tell us that it wasn't so much what we said, taught or prayed but it was how we worked together as a team and the love we had for each other which touched them.

Godly unity

Love could be seen as some sloppy emotion, but the true love of God's about being set free to be yourself and express a full range of emotions. True love gives space and time to another, honors a difference of opinion, and sets others free to question and respond. True love doesn't take offence. Team work is a powerful tool in the Lord's hands, not just to talk about unity but to live true unity, and in doing so be an intercessory *bridge* for His love to flow to those who desperately need it.

I have often said to the teams I have worked with that we are 'God with skin on'. This is not to say we try to be God and somehow rustle up perfection. No, the most powerful intercessory tool of love comes when we're truly empowered in our human weakness by our relationship with Jesus.

I have experienced differing views, misunderstandings, hurts, pains, offences, rejections and all manner of struggles in teamwork. I used to feel incredibly responsible and want to put it right in a way that came from my human way of fixing things. I have long since had to learn that God's not afraid of the mess, the negative emotion, the wrong attitudes and responses nor the words and actions which flow from them. If I had had my way, I would have tried to hide it all away so that it was neat and tidy on the outside. It has been one of the most important lessons of my intercessory walk to understand that mess has to come out into the light. In fact, I can truthfully say that when struggles have occurred and situations become messy in relationships, it's then that the Lord does His deepest work, if we allow Him to.

It's through these situations that as a team we can be truthful and real about ourselves which in turn gives permission to others to be real and honest too. Nobody would say this is easy, it isn't. In fact it's painful, but if we allow the Lord to bring His redemption, it's powerful. It's then that we invite Lord into the situation and seek His help. As children we can go to our Heavenly Father in humility and tell Him we need His help. The enemy would like to use our pretence and unreality because his plan is to keep us from truth at all costs. When we're separated from truth, it breeds mistrust and division in relationships. Unity can only be based on truth and reality. We all need the humility to allow God to do His work in us and it's the cross of Jesus which unifies us, because we all need His love, His forgiveness and His redemption in our lives.

Sadly, in the body of Christ today we see many separations. That's not to say there aren't some right separations through obvious differences of calling, function or geography, but I mean separations like the putting away of each other through offence and un-forgiveness bringing disorder and division. In God's sight each of us are different. We may have differing emphasis, experiences, abilities, upbringings and expressions. Being different in practice, viewpoint or expression is not interpreted by God as bad. He knows each one of us is sinful and inherently fallible, and yet in His heart, over-riding this, is the truth that each one of us is precious to Him and has something valuable to bring to the whole. We all have blind spots and all of us have hearts full of prejudices.

Only God, whose nature is full of mercy and justice, can expose these to us and help us to change, but He uses others to do this and sometimes puts us in uncomfortable situations and places so that we're faced with what's truly in our hearts. If the body of Christ is going to be a true expression of the healing heart of God, then we all need to learn this important intercessory lesson that God requires truth in the innermost parts of our hearts (Psalm 51:6). Otherwise we won't reflect truth and the world will rightly say we are hypocritical.

From the beginning of our ministry, God made it clear to us that there were no denominations with Him. He didn't want any of us to minister with a denominational bias to anyone. That's not to say that each denomination doesn't matter to God. They do, for they all have their own identity and strength and each one has its own value. But the intercessory work of seeing people come to healing is that we bring people into a deeper relationship with Christ Jesus as a person. As we have been obedient to the truth of Scripture that our unity lies at the cross, where we all receive forgiveness and new life and are in need of Jesus for life itself, we experience an outpouring of the love of God and His healing power.

In England someone learning to drive a car has a red 'L' for learner boldly displayed on their car. As children of God, this is exactly where we are. None of us has arrived yet, either as a person or as a Christian. There's no end to our learning and our Heavenly Father is looking for humility in us, so we can learn and grow. He has many ways of teaching us.

When we come into His kingdom some of the ways we have learnt have to be dispensed with because they're not His ways. Our Heavenly Father not only wants to show us His works but wants us to understand and enter into His ways. This is an exciting adventure if we would dare to embrace it. He calls us into team work with Him and with others.

The enemy of God on the other hand, is seeking to isolate us and divide us from one another, either through hurt and pain or attitude of heart. He does this by using fears, insecurities, past hurts and using our faulty perspectives of ourselves, of others and of God Himself. This is often the reason why teamwork is so 'contended for' and why so many Christians do become extremely independent and isolated.

One of the greatest tactics of the enemy to achieve division is to tempt us to take up an offence and harbor it in our heart and if possible to pass it on to others, so that it can be spread. This is the way the enemy would have us do his work because we absorb his nature and character by wrongly criticizing, judging and blaming which leads us to be ever fault finding and accusing. Satan is the father of all lies (John 8:44). The name Satan means *accuser* and it's his nature and character to blame, accuse and condemn us.

As human beings we're incapable of seeing into another person's heart and judging them. This is why Jesus was so clear that we must forgive and release the judgment of others to Him (Matthew

18:21-35). We're called to walk in forgiveness. Forgiveness of each other is not simply a one-off act. Rather forgiveness is a daily walk, which is dependent on walking in the grace of God through His Spirit within us.

Nothing challenges our unity more than holding offences and becoming bitter and resentful. It's here we are challenged to put our ministry to the test by taking these things to the Lord. He will bring conviction when necessary but also comfort and direct us.

Gifting and multiplication

God created us to have a balance between independence and dependence. These two truths go hand in hand. It's a question of balance. The enemy will always seek to take us to extremes and there are many who fall into the trap of becoming completely independent with an attitude of heart and mind which says, "I don't need anybody except God" or on the other end of the scale, a wrong dependence which attaches itself to others out of a deep neediness to gain value, worth and security from them. Neither of these extremes are God's way.

Teamwork is about putting all our gifting, abilities and callings together for the good of the whole body of Christ (see Ephesians chapter 4). In bringing healing to individuals, it's vital that each member of the team looks to God as their source of truth and guidance, however small they feel their part is. As individuals we are impaired in our vision, but along with others there's increased vision. No one single individual has the whole picture. We must work as a team.

Jesus called the disciples out in twos and in His divine multiplication, the kingdom grows. One and one doesn't equal two to God! He brings multiplication out of what we bring to Him. The story of the young boy bringing Jesus his own picnic of two loaves and five fishes and Jesus multiplying it for thousands gives us encouragement to do our small part and allow God to do the rest.

We have often been asked how Ellel Ministries has grown so fast. The answer is simple. As a very small team we have been obedient to God's call in ministering to the 'one', giving them life in Jesus' name. God has then given the increase and the multiplication. It can't be man's doing, it's beyond human ability and gifting. When God does something it's not possible for a human being to make it happen, even with their highest qualifications, intellect gifting, ability or even Christian experience.

We come to God as clay pots to demonstrate that this extraordinary power belongs to Him (2 Corinthians 4:7). This verse is so releasing because it takes away from us the false responsibility we can sometimes carry for God! It's always good to remember we're simply the vessel. But our role is to keep that vessel in the place where God can use it most effectively. It's a challenge to our flesh and to our humanity to be obedient to what God is asking us to do, however great or small. God may use us in a small way or in a very significant way at any given time in the team setting. God will bless us when we're teachable and humble.

I remember the team being asked to pray for a lady who was deeply into the occult. She came seeking prayer for healing of the torment in her mind. As the team was asking her questions about her problem, my eyes kept being drawn to her handbag on the floor. I finally realized that it was the Lord working to alert me to a problem this lady had. I battled with the courage to ask her what was in her handbag. Another team member encouraged me to proceed in asking the lady about this situation. My reasoning said that the thought was just in my head or mind and wasn't from God. However, I finally plucked up the courage and told her that the Lord was showing me she had something dangerous in her handbag. She looked at us all sheepishly and then fear filled her eyes. She had a grotesque, occult object wrapped up in her bag and, as she tentatively produced it to show us, she explained she had brought it *just in case*. She thought she could use it if the prayers we prayed didn't work for her.

What a learning curve this was. It had never entered my head that anyone could possibly put their trust in two separate powers, good and evil, at the same time. Praise God that she was honest enough to open her handbag and bring into the light what God had exposed. It was no wonder that she had such a great battle to repent, renounce the powers of darkness and be separated from them. Ahead lay great contention in her life as the enemy sought to pull her back into his territory.

Listening to God in this situation was vital and cut across hours of time trying to help this person and praying all the right prayers but with no seeming effect. I only played a small part in helping this lady but nevertheless it unlocked the door to the problem. The greater part of the work was done by other team members. The experience and gifting in each of us brought clarity and the way forward in her situation. Each person in the team played their part and the lady had her part to play. She had the choice whether to confess or deny the problem and a choice whether to continue on with the way forward we were showing her. If she were to receive correction and choose the way forward then the Lord would bring a powerful anointing on our corporate unity and she would receive His healing and strength and be able to continue on His way. You may sometimes feel that your part in bringing healing to someone is a small one, but a small thing can be very important.

Each of us is uniquely gifted and used by the Lord. Whether natural or spiritual gifts, each is vital and will be used under God's hand to bring in His purposes. This is how He designed mankind. In His love He made us with diversity of personality and gifting. When we come to Him through Jesus, He further gifts us with the power of His Holy Spirit indwelling us. Through Him, we can exercise the gifts of the Holy Spirit and display the fruit of the Holy Spirit in our lives.

Separate yet corporate

Our right need of each other in teamwork brings about the blessing of God our Father. When we affirm and value and trust God in each other, it releases the power of God to bring change. Incredibly, we empower Him to empower us! It's a natural response of a parent to a child. We see this in the natural realm. Parents pour out blessings on their children, when those children are being a blessing to them. In a practical way, this often means working through differing opinions and different perspectives but if we're looking to God to bring the breakthrough, He can do it. God will use all the perspectives and even differing opinions.

In the healing environment when ministering to someone, I have seen how one team member may be aware of the person's hurt and is ministering the compassion and love of Christ into this place. Another team member has been aware of the person's desire to give up and make a strong inner vow never to trust anyone or open up and be vulnerable again. Another team member believes strong confrontation is necessary and yet another believes reading a passage of Scripture holds the key. It has always been very encouraging for me that God in His wisdom can bring about His purposes for the person despite us and our imperfections. Somehow in the midst of all our perspectives, God's doing His work through us and each has a piece to bring to the whole picture.

There are no perfections in team work. God's not looking for perfect people. Sometimes, what comes from us seems empty faith and words or powerless prayers. Sometimes our feelings seem to be unspiritual and we don't sense any anointing! I remember once praying what I thought was the most awful, un-anointed and uninspired prayer, only to find that the person I was praying for was deeply moved and with tears running down their face they responded to God in a meaningful way. On the other hand, I have often prayed what I felt was my most anointed prayer with passion and even with tears, and the person I have prayed for feels nothing and there's little response.

I once received a letter from someone years after I had apparently prayed for them at a healing service. I had long forgotten the person and the prayer I prayed. They wrote to say how much that time of prayer had meant to them and how their life had been transformed and healed. As I began to recall the situation, I also recalled how disappointed I was at the time that nothing had happened. It was an important lesson to me to realize that my work was obedience and I needed to leave the outcome to God. His timing is not our timing.

One of the traps we can fall into is to be over-critical of each other rather than looking at what God can do through each of us. When I was ministry manager at Ellel Grange, it was my job along with others to select the ministry team. We had a wonderful team of people who had a great heart to help others. We hold three-day healing retreats at all our centers and have done so since the beginning of the ministry. The ministry teams work in pairs and each pair prays with an individual for around two to three hours.

There came a time when I was beginning to think a certain couple was completely unsuitable for this type of work. They were limited in their understanding and had physical disabilities too. They were also quite naïve, and yet they loved the Lord and loved His people. However, I began to believe that these people needed to use their gifting elsewhere and I thought to myself privately that I wouldn't like either of these two to minister to me. As I was praying about how I would approach the couple to tell them of my verdict as kindly as I could, a testimony letter came in from someone on the retreat. Their whole letter was full of praise for this couple and how God had used them. I had been busily pouring out my exasperations with the various ministry team people we had. I had been telling the Lord of their limitations and apparent insensitivity. In fact, if I had had my way at that stage, I would have eliminated a large part of the team. God spoke with me and lovingly said, "yes and I would have eliminated you as well."

Oh dear! How I needed this lesson, that God will use who He will use. Man looks on the outward appearance but God looks on the heart. The most important work we have to do is to bring people to the place where they are looking to God to do His work through a human channel and not looking to man.

Clay pots

Another principle I have learnt in seeing intercessory breakthrough in teamwork is that God doesn't share His glory with another. Humankind was not designed or built to be glory-takers. In fact our human nature would move into pride and arrogance and we all know that pride goes before a fall. Pride separates us from God. This was the sin of Adam and Eve. They thought they knew better, could do it better on their own and control their own life and destiny separate from their creator. In essence they elevated themselves above God by not trusting Him.

We do well when we learn the lesson of pride and seek to open our hearts in humility and trust towards our Heavenly Father. If we don't learn to identify pride and its consequences in our lives, our flesh could easily move away from God down a track of our own making which might seem good but which has left God behind. We would then be vulnerable to taking the glory for ourselves which is the ultimate and worst outworking of the sin of pride. We need to develop a holy fear of taking God's glory for ourselves.

The intercessory role is on behalf of another and as we seek God in this place, it's vital to give God all the glory for what He has done. He's the potter and we're the clay. As we remember this, our part in any of the action is put into the right perspective. We have this treasure in clay pots (2 Corinthians 4:7). As a team we constantly have to ask the Lord to help us not to make *'flesh our arm'* (Jeremiah 17:5) and if we have in any way, we ask Him to bring us back to Him and to dependency upon Him. It's so easy to begin something in submission to God and to end up doing it ourselves and not notice we have left God behind.

Praise God that He didn't make us angels and nor did He make us divine. He made us human beings with very real flesh. He knows our needs and our greatest need is of Him as our Father. Our goal is to know more of Him and to lead others to as well. It's in knowing Him that we find ourselves, our God-given personality which is so precious to Him and our sinful nature which needs weeding out and putting to death, for it won't go with us when we go to glory and it will entangle and snare us here on earth if given the chance. We have been given the tools and the power of God over the works of darkness which seek to steal and spoil our destiny, personality, gifting and our very life.

Family

When we come to Jesus, we become sons and heirs with Him in our Father's inheritance. In other words, we become part of His family. We belong to Him. A healthy family is a team whose members believe in each other, prefer each other, watch over each other and above all have great love and pride in their Father.

When the work of Ellel Ministries began, the Lord made it clear to us that we were His family and people who came to be healed needed to understand that and enter into 'family' above all else. So began what turned out to be the largest battle of all. Satan hates family. It's the opposite of everything in his character.

God created family and the human race was designed for family. The Church is a family. It's not buildings. Living as a family is greatly contended over and yet it's the highest calling. The body of Christ today is meant to be a healing body, one that expresses and lives out the heart of God for one other.

People have often asked us why we needed such seemingly 'grand' buildings for the ministry God has called us to. We believe it was so much on the heart of God to provide a place which would be 'home' for His family. He wanted to meet with them in a place where they could let down their guard and defenses and be real with Him and have time with Him.

Through this, the extraordinary began to happen. The Lord was meeting with people through the meal times, through the love and sense of family, through times of fun and through times of mutual pain and reality. As human beings, we all have needs and there are times when we have great struggles and pain. The cross of Jesus levels us all. It doesn't matter whether we're rich or poor, Greek or Jew, young or old. Neither does it matter what our gifts or abilities are or what kind of upbringing we have had.

Human suffering and need is universal. We all need love, family and belonging. People began to say that they had experienced love and safety. A unity began to emerge both in the team and in those who came for help and training, which was beyond anything we could imagine. People didn't want to leave. A tangible 'taste of heaven' was felt as deep bonds were forged in and through the love of God. Those with broken hearts came and received deep healing. Many who come through the doors of Ellel Ministries centers worldwide have never experienced true family and they enter into the best healing of all – that of knowing who they are and why they exist. Identity and destiny begin to unfold in people's lives through the love of God and His family.

If we could say anything was the key to the anointing people see on the work of Ellel Ministries, it would be that God has called us to be family and as we continue to express this in terms of loving and serving one another, healing will take place and the kingdom of God will grow. This isn't to say it will be easy. Truth and reality have to be at the core. This will mean that issues have to be brought to the surface and faced. To be in God's family or team means being built on true love, not on false love which pretends, manipulates, covers up or is selfish.

At the heart of intercession is team work. Satan would divide us but God's plan is to unite us as one that we become a welcoming and healing family which characterizes our Father and displays His attributes. If we live our lives from this place, there will be no limits to what God will accomplish for His kingdom and we'll all be the bearers of much fruit.

Godly Order, Authority and Power

Authority belongs to God. He is the creator and author of all authority and the power that flows from it. Before mankind sinned and turned their back on God's authority, there was a perfect trust that God's ways were right. The serpent came and tempted man to doubt God and to be disobedient to the commands of God.

We all know the consequence of this disobedience. As a result sin and death entered the world and the human race and from thereon in, a battle for authority commenced. Satan is jealous for all that belongs to God and contends for it. He wants God's authority and he seeks the co-operation and agreement of mankind against the will of God in order to achieve this goal. With sin and rebellion sown into our hearts, we now have to battle against yielding to the flesh and the enemy. We struggle to submit to God's ways and His truth.

Authority is something which has to be *given*, it's not something that can legitimately be *taken*, although it is possible to steal authority and use it wrongly. It's also possible to give authority away in a wrong way. Adam and Eve submitted to Satan in eating the forbidden fruit, and so gave away authority to Satan – the authority which God had given to *them*. When rightful authority is either stolen or given away, all manner of disorder comes about as a result. There will be a progression of ungodly domination, manipulation and control taking the place of the trusting relationship God originally intended.

God intended authority to be a place of safety. Without this protection, humankind is vulnerable to the schemes and devices of the enemy of souls. His purpose is to steal the authority God has given to us and in a progressive way to take us further and further away from God's truth and power and into his lies and dominion.

Our prayerful and intercessory role is to take our place in this battle and to take back from the enemy all that has been stolen, both from us personally, but most crucially that which has been stolen from God. When the enemy steals our hearts or part of our lives, he robs God. He is a destiny-robber. In robbing us of our potential he's stealing the fruitfulness God intended for us. God's glory is being stolen.

The Scripture tells us that the human heart is *'deceitful and wicked above all things'* (Jeremiah 17:19). Our hearts deceive us and the pride of man would want to take all the credit and glory for what man sees he has achieved. There is a rightful pride (value and self worth) in what we have seen accomplished through our own work. However, there is also the truth that nothing of what we have achieved could have been done without God. He is the Creator. He gave us the gifting and enabling. Without Him, we would not be who we are or even have life itself. Therefore it's vital that, as created beings, we give our thanks and praise and worship to our creator God, who is our Father.

It's out of the love of our hearts and obedience to our Father in Heaven that we submit to His ways and give Him the glory, so that His name is honored and we receive blessing as His children. It's a subtle temptation, but very easy, to take the glory of God to ourselves. We can take it to build ourselves up - our reputation, our power base and sadly, even our kingdom. Incredible though it may seem it's easy to be so deceived that we do this in God's *name*.

Young children usually are able to learn when their father is acting in their best interests and although they may not fully understand the reasoning, they trust and feel safe in their father's care and protection. Even in small children, the rebellious carnal nature rises up to take control of its own way. Any mother or father will tell us this is dangerous, for small children don't have an adequate framework for danger. They can't see what their parents can see and they don't know the consequences that their parents know about.

Our nature as grown-up individuals remains inherently rebellious. In relationship with our heavenly Father, it's imperative that we deal with pride and submit to His authority, both in our own lives and in the ministry he has called us to.

Our sinful hearts hate submission. In essence we are all guilty of the original sin of Adam and Eve. We want to do it our way! Many people will have heard of the famous Frank Sinatra song with the line, '*I did it my way*'. God allows us to have our own free will choices within parameters. Walking within these boundaries gives us safety. If we are to be effective in the kingdom of God, it's important for us to know these boundaries of His kingdom, so that we remain in safety under His covering and blessing.

God works with order, and answered prayer will follow when we learn to discern this and walk in His principles. God has not called us to be loners but to be submitted to each other and to God-given authority over us. When we are working in teams to bring an intercessory breakthrough on behalf of another person, it is vital we understand authority. If we don't, we will never be able to exercise God-given authority over the power of the enemy. To *exercise* godly authority, we need to be *under* godly authority.

It would be foolish for any individual to set themselves up to minister to someone's healing needs without being under some spiritual authority. This means ministering with the approval and blessing of the spiritual authority you are under - a church minister or a leader in a Christian organization.

The structure in Ellel Ministries

In Ellel Ministries, we have a well-defined structure and order. Each center has its own ministry manager who is under the authority of the center director. The center director is under the authority of 'the Executive Leadership' of Ellel Ministries. Authority is granted to each person on the ministry team to pray for those who come to the center through a well-defined practice and order. Safeguards are in place. For example, it's made clear that authority is only given for the ministry team to pray for people within the center itself and with the full knowledge of the ministry manager.

Anyone who wants to undertake ministry in another place, in someone's home for example, would not be covered by Ellel Ministries. God gave this principle as a safe boundary for the ministry of healing and it has resulted in unprecedented blessing. We have experienced all manner of disorder when people who were trusted with authority to pray for others didn't come under rightful authority themselves. The power of the enemy was able to see an opening in those circumstances and demons began their work to divide and bring destruction.

I recall one person who didn't agree with what he viewed as irrelevant authority issues within the structure of the ministry. He had been put in place for good reasons through prayerful consideration by experienced leaders within the work. Yet this person had been a leader in a local church and he felt he knew better. He ignored the safeguards and conditions and secretly carried out his own agenda.

As a result, the team became confused about the authority within the work and who they should obey instructions from. Division became inevitable. Praise God for those who were praying and interceding and were alerted that the enemy was seeking to bring about destruction through one person's rebellion to authority. Godly leadership had to bring exposure and correction - never an easy thing to do. Nobody likes confrontation but it brought about cleansing - the fruit of repentance. Peace returned and the enemy was thwarted.

Godly authority in human vessels

People who come for healing prayer may need help in understanding that they are receiving from God, but He's using a human vessel. In submitting and yielding themselves to God's chosen vessel, they will be enabling God to bring a powerful anointing of His Spirit. It's vital to help them see that they aren't so much looking to a person for help, although the fact that God uses a person to help them *is* an important principle. They should understand that the team are looking to God too. In this way, there will be a continuous flow of God's anointing. The alternative is a horizontal (and possibly 'soulish') encounter, with answers sought or given only out of human affection, compassion or experience.

It's my experience that as we encourage the person we are helping to look to God, and we ourselves look to God, the Lord will in some unique way fill our minds with a thought, a conviction, a prayer, or an insight which is the key to a breakthrough in this person's life. His divine authority is released to us in a supernatural way in the prayer room. As we humbly submit to God, we can all receive from Him.

We may receive a word of correction to give. We must help people to receive confrontation and correction through us as human channels, trusting that God will use us to speak that which is on His heart into their lives. Broken and damaged people will find submission hard and yet without walking this way, they will never be able to yield to God. God has chosen to use human vessels to be channels of His authority and power even though they are fallible. This is His way of bringing about structure and order into the world we live in. If we rightly submit to human authority, God will bless.

Some say, "I only obey God" or "God told me". But when they become the sole source of hearing God, without anyone else weighing and testing their guidance, they open the door to deception. They are becoming their own authority and source of truth. We all need each other in order to receive a balance of truth. In His love, God has placed people in spiritual authority over us. They can often see truths we ourselves can't.

When we are exercising an authority role, it's essential that we are *under* human authority. Some people tell us that they only come under *God's* authority. I once encountered someone who had a completely deceptive vision. This person was adamant that the vision was from God and she "could not let our unbelief get in the way of what God was telling her". Sadly, this kind of situation gives place for the enemy to play havoc with people. They are very sincere. But it's possible to be sincerely deceived.

God blesses order in team work and it's part of His purpose in safeguarding us from the enemy. We ignore this at our peril. We also need to realize that our prideful hearts would always tell us we are right and others who disagree with us are wrong and will stop the submitting of ourselves to accountability for our decisions and actions.

In a team setting it is godly order for there to be a team leader. This person gives leadership and is accountable to God. He or she is also accountable to others, together in leadership. Being a leader doesn't mean being more important to God, rather it means being held more accountable. A position of leadership should not be taken lightly. When ministering healing to others, a team perspective is vital. It is part of God's plan. The same principles apply in any type of intercession - we must all be under human authority and accountable to others. That is why we are called the body of Christ.

When our heart motive and intentions are right, God blesses and brings good out of our weaknesses and even our mistakes. God can't bless where there's disunity and disorder. The enemy uses these two areas to his advantage. For the anointing of God to flow in power, we mustn't let issues divide us. This doesn't mean that we always have to be in agreement, but that there's a right place and a right way to express our disagreement and then we have to leave the rest to God. He's the One who judges those placed in authority.

If you are the one in authority then you have a privileged role in bringing those you are helping into a safe place. Authority should never be a weapon or be used for power or prideful purposes. Authority is a servant role. Jesus was the servant King and He served those He helped sacrificially. He always safeguarded their dignity.

Wherever confrontation is needed in the intercessory role, it needs to be brought without personal prejudice and with the heart of God clearly expressed. God hates sin, He sees what it does to us and in His love He exposes it so that we can deal with it and come into freedom. The Holy Spirit convicts us of sin so that we can turn from destructive ways into fruitful ways leading to life.

Godly authority safeguards the people under their care from danger. Sadly there are many people who are fearful of authority, having been deeply hurt as a result of authority being wrongly used upon them. Many in authority do use their power wrongly. They received a model of authority which was wrong and have been damaged and hurt themselves.

It is essential if we are those who are exercising authority that we do so from a *healed place*. Much damage is done in the name of God by those who bring domination and cause fear. But we should also remember that authority can often be 'perceived' as wrong by those who have unhealed areas in their own lives. It's all too easy for hurting people to believe the motive of others is to hurt them.

God is looking for men and women who are after His own heart and will be His hands and feet, eyes and ears and arms outstretched to others. He gives us a great example of His way of exercising authority through the New Testament parable of the Lost Sheep. The Great Shepherd of the sheep (Jesus) left the ninety-nine to look for the one which had gone astray. His motivation was love and mercy. He knew the danger the lost sheep was in.

The Great Shepherd eventually found the sheep and used His Shepherd's crook to save it. This wasn't soft and sentimental love. The Shepherd used the crook as an instrument of authority over the stupidity, stubbornness and self will of the sheep. In fact the sheep may well have received some bruising as a result of the battle to free it from the thicket and bring it back from danger. Loving authority will not spare us if it means bringing some hurt and pain but with the motive of ultimately rescuing us from danger.

If we are going to be those who effectively bring rescue and help for others, we will need to move in the love and mercy of God and bring His authority into people's lives through exercising godly confrontation. As a result we will see the enemy of souls

Angelic Help

When we bring others into the restoring and healing heart of God, we are ministering salvation to them. In other words we are applying the work of the cross into their lives so that they may be transformed and enabled to live the abundant life Jesus came to bring (John 10:10). This is discipleship and healing. It's part of what salvation means. In this intercessory role we can be sure that the Lord wants us to look to Him for angelic help (Hebrews 1:14).

A full explanation goes beyond the scope of this book but Scripture is clear that there are spiritual battles in the heavenly realms between the angels of the Lord and the demonic powers (Revelation chapter 12). Although these heavenly realms are opposite in nature they are not to be thought of as equal in any way. We know that the victory in Christ is assured. It has already been won. Jesus finished the work of defeating the powers of darkness when He willingly gave up His life to die on the cross.

> *When Jesus had received the wine, he said, "It is finished." Then He bowed His head and gave up His spirit.*
>
> (John 19:30).

> *Our struggle is not against enemies of blood and flesh, but against the rulers, against the authorities, against the cosmic powers of this*

present darkness, against the spiritual forces of evil in the heavenly places.

(Ephesians 6:12)

In order for us to understand the battle we are in and gain the victory, we need to find out what is at our disposal. Chapter 6 of Ephesians exhorts us to be sure we wear the armor of God. We will look at this in a later chapter.

In order to understand angelic help we must also understand something of the spiritual battle there is in the heavenly realms, referred to by Scripture. Demonic powers are not fanciful thoughts and ideas but are real spiritual beings which Jesus defeated on our behalf. The enemy of God, Satan, is himself deceived into believing he is capable of stealing all that belongs to God. It's our role, as disciples of Jesus, to plunder Satan's kingdom of darkness and usher in God's kingdom of light and truth.

There are three ways in which Satan's kingdom can be effectively plundered. The first way is through our own lives being under the Lordship of Jesus. The second way, (which follows from the first because it means we are seated with Jesus in heavenly places), is through exercising God-given authority over the powers of darkness. The third way is through our prayers and intercession as we participate in releasing the purposes of God here on earth.

I want now to look more closely at some keys to understanding angelic help and intervention.

Angels and free will

God has given His disciples authority over the demonic. In the name of Jesus, we can command the demonic to leave. Jesus has won the victory over demons and we are in Jesus. From this position we have been given authority over them. However, we do *not* have authority over another person's free will. We can't say, for instance, "I bind your will and intentions in the name of Jesus." Neither does Jesus take authority over a person's free-will choices.

Jesus tells us the way and leads us into a place of safety. He is our Shepherd and King. As His people, we have freely chosen to follow Him as the Shepherd and live under His rule and reign as the King. God never overrides our free will. We give Him Lordship and permission to reign in our lives. He doesn't force us to do anything but His Word does tell us the consequences we will suffer if we disobey Him.

In most circumstances, when one human violates another person's free will, ungodly power will be unleashed which the enemy can use. However, there are some situations where it is right and godly to override human will. For instance when a people break the laws of the land and needs to be arrested or when people have lost their sanity and it's necessary to override their free will in order to keep them or others safe.

In order to claim the victory Jesus has won for us, we need to take a closer look at the order God has put into His kingdom so that we remain under His safety and protection. The issue of free will is the key.

We have all been given God's gift of free will and nowhere in Scripture does it give us any indication that we have any authority over another's free will. We can advise, exhort, confront and even give orders and instructions but the person has to come to the place where they freely agree and obey.

We would be going outside God's intended order for life if, in a determined and deliberate way, we took away another person's free will. This would be using domination, manipulation and control - which are the fundamental ways that Satan uses to gain access into people's lives. Maybe we have received domination, manipulation and control ourselves and it has left us vulnerable to Satan.

I once ministered to a lady and found out that every choice she made was on the basis of fear. When she was a child, her parents were unable to put into her the right framework of confidence and security to make decisions that would be appropriate to her growing years. She was continually treated as a robot, being told what she liked or disliked, what suited her or what didn't, where she should go and where she should not go.

Her parents were full of fear and constantly panicked that she would come to harm if she fell or had an accident when she was playing. For this reason she was kept 'safe', seemingly out of harm's way and away from playgrounds, play areas or friends of the same age.

She was kept in a prison with tight boundaries, which did far more damage than allowing her the freedom to play, experiment, adventure and explore. Every child needs to do these things in order to grow and develop as an individual person. The outcome was that although this lady was extremely intelligent and had a professional career, on the inside her emotions were undeveloped and like those of a small child.

She had never learnt to be secure in choosing, making mistakes, learning and growing. She would panic and have deep level anxiety when she had to make a decision. Her lifestyle choices were severely distorted and disabled.

All her decisions were taken to avoid situations she was insecure about, and hence many obsessions and phobias had arisen in her life. At the age of thirty nine, she was still looking to her mother to tell her what to do. Consequently when she had her own children, they too were dominated by her fear and didn't receive the necessary freedom to develop their own free will and grow, with the ability to be spontaneous, to adventure and explore. Every choice was based on their mother's controlling fear and the need to make everything absolutely safe.

In complete contrast to having parents who tried to keep her safe, I once ministered to a lady who had been treated very cruelly. She was dominated by the fear of punishment. If she made the smallest mistake, such as accidentally dropping food on the floor as a child, she was beaten or locked up. The punishment throughout her childhood was harsh and unjust. The domination in this case was more obviously fuelled by demonic power.

In both of these cases, fear was used to dominate God's precious gift of free will within the child. The end result in each person was very severe bondage and crippling, leading to a lifetime of depression and struggle. The good news is that in the name of Jesus they received freedom and healing.

Whenever domination (as opposed to right authority) is used to control people, the enemy of souls is given power. Domination is manipulative and in severe cases of domination, it exercises powerful control over others, particularly in the area of their free will.

A young man came for help as he had severe problems with a phobia. The phobia manifested itself in claustrophobia – a fear of enclosed spaces. Through prayer ministry, it was evident that the fear had come in through his being tightly controlled by a very dominating mother. The mother was highly critical of him as a child and he was continuously corrected. The mother's disapproval of him had started when he was conceived because she hated the man who had made her pregnant.

The mother's guilt and shame at bearing a son out of wedlock, and to a man she hated, compounded guilt and feelings of hatred towards her child. This resulted in ambivalence in her attitude and emotions. At one level she desperately loved and wanted her child, but on another subconscious level she hated his gender and looks. They reminded her of the man she hated and through whom she had become pregnant. This hatred was transferred onto the child. As the son grew up, the mother became more and more malicious. She had bouts of emotional and physical cruelty towards the growing boy.

As a man coming for help, he was very conscious of his mother's voice and control dominating his personhood. His pent up fury and anger was becoming increasingly uncontrolled and he was in danger of this destroying both himself and any possible relation ship with a future partner. He had turned to substance abuse as a way of holding back his feelings.

Apart from the need for emotional healing and help, there was a real need for this young man to receive spiritual help, to free him from the powers unleashed against him. These were not just to do with the past issues but the ongoing daily issues he faced as his mother continued to try to control and dominate his life.

The bible speaks of hatred being the same as murder (Matthew 5:21-22) and the ongoing malice of the young man's mother meant he was continuously under spiritual attack, even though he was physically separated.

He spoke occasionally of sensing his mother's presence and her oppression of him. During times of prayer where he was helped to forgive and to receive healing for his difficult and traumatic past, he came into great release. However, there remained times when it appeared he was overtaken by an irrational quaking fear of an impending doom. It was when the ministry team prayed and asked the Lord Jesus to send His angels to warfare on behalf of the young man by taking away the element of his mother's human spirit maliciously aimed towards him, that he came into deeper freedom.

Curses - of words, thoughts and intent - were being used against this young man. They were powerful because this man was vulnerable emotionally to his mother. As a child he fearfully submitted to her every whim. Now as an adult, he could reason that this should not be so, but the years of programming from childhood coming from her demands and domination did not just go away. Satan had a real stronghold over his formative development.

This is how witchcraft works. It uses domination, manipulation and control to gain the submission of another person's free will. Once there has been submission through intimidation, fear and guilt, witchcraft has done the work, in gaining the captive's willingness, through fear, to submit.

We came to understand that when we are dealing with an ungodly intent being targeted towards an individual or group of individuals, we need to ask the Lord Jesus to send His angels to assist us in the battle.

We learnt to pray prayers asking the Lord to separate the human power from the demonic power. We used our authority to bind the demonic power. We then asked the Lord to release His angelic host to remove the projected human power from the person we were seeking to help. Following this prayer, we found that deliverance came much more easily and then came the fuller freedom for the person to find themselves and their own identity.

Angels' participation in the battle

The Heavenly Host is a magnificently ordered group who do the Lord's bidding. There are warfare angels such as Michael (Revelation 12:7) and there are also messenger angels such as Gabriel (Luke 1:26). We can also be sure that there are ministering angels who help with the Lord's work (Hebrews 1:14). All the angelic host are deployed in response to the prayers of the saints. I want to emphasize here that these prayers should be addressed to God, not directly to the angels.

We are called to be soldiers in the Lord's army. An army is well disciplined with rank and file and obeys standing orders. If intercession is to be effective, we will learn how to take our place as soldiers of the Lord Jesus Christ and in His army. Along with the Heavenly Host, we will experience many victories.

If, on the other hand, we never truly learn what it is to be a soldier then we can be tossed about in a sea of trying to make sense of life, its struggles, battles and confusions. The spiritual forces of darkness will ensure that our lives are less than fruitful and that the kingdom of God doesn't grow.

Scripture is clear that we have authority over the demonic powers. Through the finished work of the cross, we are joined to Christ in our salvation and are seated with Him in Heavenly places. We are in Him and He is in us. Jesus was never subject to sin or death. He voluntarily gave up His life in an act of love to die for the sins of mankind and therefore never came under the god of this world, who is Satan. Jesus is seated over the powers of darkness and has won all authority over them. Jesus gave His disciples His power and His authority to cast out demons in His name (Luke 9:1-2).

In Him, we have the right and authority to command the powers of darkness to leave in the name of Jesus. However, it's vital we understand that a person's free will can give demons rights to remain if the person is not willing to come in submission to Christ in certain areas of their life. When this is the case, there will be no point using our authority because the darkness will have rights to remain until the person's repentance and free will is engaged. We will need to pray for the person to see the truth and light and for the Holy Spirit to bring conviction and empowering for a change of heart.

Just as we have no authority over the free will of a person, neither do we have authority over the angelic beings. Scripture is clear that we must ask the Lord to send the angels. They are at His bidding alone and in certain situations God does release His Heavenly Host to help us.

Angels in situations of occult power being unleashed

I remember being in a ministry situation which was dealing with high occult power. From time to time, the room felt cold. The battles would be intense as the evil powers which had rights in the person's life raged. We would cry out to the Lord in prayer for help as it seemed we had no power to break through in the situation. It was an unforgettable experience when the person concerned spoke out and said she could see angels in the room, and indeed there was a tangible presence of the anointing of the Lord. From that time on the battle lessened and our prayers were effective. The victory was sweet and came with great rejoicing.

We learnt to thank the Lord for the heavenly host which accompanied the breakthrough. In fact, this became a normal part of our praying. We asked the Lord to release His heavenly host to assist us in the work of bringing salvation and rescue. We thanked Him for doing so and for the part they have played in bringing victory.

On another occasion we had a person who had lived her life bound by witchcraft powers. These powers did not want to see her set free and would contend for her life. On the surface she seemed suicidal but assured us she was desperate to live. In her desperation and broken-ness there was a day when the demonic powers were taunting her so much that her strength gave way and she was about to be in great danger by physically running away.

We asked the Lord to send His angels to help us in the battle. To our amazement we witnessed her elbows being drawn to her knees so that she could not physically move! We were then able to identify the problem and see her set free.

Angelic help where there is sickness, disease or death

A lady came to us with a great sadness in her life. She had been married for eleven years and was desperate for a child. She had been to many places for prayer but to no avail. As we were talking with her about the possibility of there being a spirit of death operating on her generation line, she began to feel physically sick.

We prayed there and then for deliverance to take place and she ran to her room to vomit! We visited her afterwards and she was lying on her bed feeling very weak. She told us she could see an angel and she needed to remain lying on the bed. We prayed with her and left the Lord to do the rest.

With great joy she wrote to us a few months later to tell us she was pregnant and had conceived straight away following her ministry. The couple's beautiful baby girl was born nine months later. They then went on to have more children. We began to understand that there were ministering angels as well as warfare angels.

Linda was a young lady aged 26 whose back had been badly broken and consequently she was disabled for life and on a disability pension. She was, as a result, extremely depressed and suicidal. It took some courage to pray for her, particularly as this was in a public setting and in front of many medics. She needed a miracle!

We began to pray through the usual issues of forgiveness and repentance, (which need to be considered during prayer for healing). Memories surfaced of the day the accident happened and Linda shuddered with fear. We asked the Lord to bring out the trauma which was embedded in her spirit and soul and to set her free from the deep shock of falling 30 feet over a cliff onto jagged rocks. She had been on a night hike with her youth club.

It was when we anointed her with oil for physical healing, that her body began to move. She had been lying on the floor while we prayed for her but suddenly her legs began to stretch out, her arms were being lifted and her back began to straighten.

She lay there under the anointing of the Holy Spirit receiving her healing and all the time this was happening it was as if angels were working on her body inside and out. It is now ten years since she received this miraculous healing. She signed off her lifetime disability pension and is now happily married with children.

I have been with quite a few people when they were dying. Mostly this has been from cancer but I'm sure the principle applies to many other situations. I have found that in the deepest times of suffering, the Lord is very close and also that He is present with His heavenly host. I truly believe that if we ask the Lord to release His angels (remembering again we do not have authority over angels, only the Lord can send them), He will do so to help in a variety of ways.

For instance the Lord will release angelic beings to minister and bring relief and comfort to those suffering from pain, the effects of drugs and various treatments. Scripture tells us that each child has its angel (Matthew 18:10). As such we can be confident that the Lord wants to use His angelic host to help us.

I have experienced the presence of angels when I have been with those who were passing from this life and going home to glory. I have also heard stories from those who were in these situations, speaking of either seeing or being aware of angels around them.

I have been involved in seeing people close to death, suffering greatly and who were ready to meet their Lord. It felt right to ask the Lord to send His angels to take the person home. It has been an awesome experience to find that without delay, the person immediately died!

We can ask the Lord to send His angels at the right time to escort our friends and loved ones 'home' to Himself. Our going home to be with the Lord is sad for those of us being left behind here on earth but it is cause for great rejoicing in the heavens when a saint passes through to glory. Psalm 116:15 says *'precious to the Lord is the death of His saints'*.

The angels have a vital role here and as intercessors we can take up our authority over demonic beings and command them to be held back and bound from bringing torment, pain, fear, and confusion. We are also quite within our rights to ask the Lord to release His angels to come and assist us in warfare and to minister to and help those who are in need. In this area we will see dramatic answers to prayer!

In our intercessory role, we should be aware that the Lord will send His angels when the situation is right for them to be there and that we can ask the Lord to send them. They are not under our command (unlike the demonic beings) but under the Lord's command.

When praying with people who are vulnerable, we ask the Lord to send His angels to guard them and minister to them. This prayer can be particularly effective at night when the person feels alone and the enemy crouches. They are a sign of the Lord's presence and they bring comfort and peace. The angels can also do supernatural acts if the Lord directs them to do so and in certain circumstances it may indeed be the right thing to ask the Lord to send angels to help.

Our prayers and our wills coming into line with the will and purpose of the Lord, strengthens the heavenly host to do their work. This is a mystery but it's something of divine team work which brings the purposes of God down here to earth. We strengthen the role of the angels by our prayers and our lives laid down in the purposes of God and this releases God's power here on earth to help us in ushering in His will.

This chapter on angels could not be complete without reference to Psalm 91, which is such an encouragement to us all as we continue the Lord's work here on earth.

Because you have made the Lord your refuge, the Most High your dwelling place, no evil shall befall you, no scourge come near your tent. For he will command his angels concerning you to guard you in all your ways. On their hands they will bear you up, so that you will not dash your foot against a stone...

Those who love me, I will deliver; I will protect those who know my name. When they call to me, I will answer them; I will be with them in trouble, I will rescue them and honor them. With long life I will satisfy them and show them my salvation."

Psalm 91:9-12, and 14-16, (NRSV)

These are precious promises from the Lord. They are not ones we should take for granted and they do indicate conditions. Our response is to love God with all our hearts and to trust Him with everything we are. We can then call on His name and He will help us. His angelic heavenly host are part of that help.

Caution when considering the angelic

It would be wrong not to mention in this chapter the need for real caution in our response to angels. As humans, it's very easy to become excited at the supernatural, especially when as Christians we become desperate to see and experience the Lord at work in this way.

In our desperation or in our desire to see the miraculous or supernatural intervention, we can be caught up in a deception. The enemy is a master deceiver. He counterfeits the work of the Lord at every opportunity. The prime way the enemy achieves his objective in this regard is to appeal to our carnal nature.

Adam and Eve were tempted by the serpent in the garden to go beyond that which God intended. God did not put up a brick wall which made this impossible. God allowed Adam and Eve to use their free will to choose to stay within the instruction that He had given them.

So it is the same today, there is no brick wall which prevents us from going further than God intended but there is grave danger that we will do so nevertheless. God has set a limit for mankind and safe boundaries for us. However, man has a nature that wants to go further.

Today we see a plethora of ways in which the enemy is tempting us into the supernatural. The good that God wants to give us is even being used by Satan to tempt us to extremes. Conversely Satan may use fear to stop us entering any supernatural experiences whatsoever.

We should beware of fascination. Satan appeals to our attraction to something which fascinates us, gives us a sense of excitement, of thrill or of power.

Satan also appeals to our need. Hurt, damaged and needy people will have a tremendous desire for significance. Having been downtrodden, their overriding need is to *be* someone. Jesus wants to bring them rightful significance but He will not perform supernatural signs or give spiritual gifts in order to give personal worth and significance. If He did, our identity would be in the sign or in the gift rather than in our humanity. If the gift or sign left us then there would be no identity.

The abundant life Jesus came to bring doesn't depend on gifting or signs but on our relationship with Jesus Himself. Satan is a master deceiver in that he is the one who would give signs and supernatural gifts in order to build a false significance and worth into a needy individual.

The world as we experience it today is full of false supernatural beliefs, cures, comforts and objects of spirituality. The world has woken up to the fact that angels are significant. Some are turning to angels as though they were mini gods to be followed, listened to and obeyed. They are being wrongly used as comforters and healers.

Demonic beings in the service of Satan can masquerade as 'good' spirits and also appear as angels, but they are false. In 2 Corinthians 11:14-15, it says, *'and no wonder! Even Satan disguises himself as an angel of light. So it is not strange if his ministers also disguise themselves as ministers of righteousness. Their end will match their deeds'.*

Counterfeit spirituality is rife. If we worship the angelic, give them position or power in our lives to lead and guide us, we will be inviting demonic spirits pretending to be God's angels, to lead us astray.

Let us thank God for His angelic host but always seek to give the glory to the Lord and to draw attention to His victory won for us at Calvary.

Praise and Worship

The greatest key to effective intercession is praise and worship. The Lord loves the humility, the trust and the adoration of His children. His heart is moved when we come to Him as Father and thank Him for His Son Jesus and ask Him to empower us by His Holy Spirit.

In touching lives which have been deeply broken and damaged, we become an intercessory *bridge* for people to be able to receive hope and restoration. Their spirits are often so weakened by the battles and struggles that life brings, that as a consequence they have been unable to lift their heads towards the Lord. Depression and oppression have dug deep into their inner being.

So this is why we begin ministry times with inviting the Lord's presence through our praise and worship. Our intercessory role is modeling something of our relationship with the Lord and how it is that they can walk with Him and see Him accomplish wonderful things in their lives.

The prayer of worship

The Psalms are the best place to go when we look for the model of prayer. David knew how to be intimate with His God.

Let us go to His dwelling place; let us worship at his footstool
Psalm 132:7

Extol the Lord our God; worship at his footstool; Holy is He.

Psalm 99:5

I like to pray something like this; "Lord we love and adore You. You are everything to us. We magnify You. We lift Your name on high. You are the One we worship and trust today."

Worship is the act of laying our lives in submission before the Lord and acknowledging Him as Lord.

The prayer of praise

Enter his gates with thanksgiving, and his courts with praise. Give thanks to him, bless his name. For the Lord is good; his steadfast love endures forever, and his faithfulness to all generations.

Psalm 100:4-5

I might pray along these lines for example, "Lord we praise You today. You are good! We praise You for bringing our friend John here today. We praise You that You have a plan for his life, that You are here by Your spirit to help and uphold him. We praise You in advance for all You are going to give him today of Yourself."

As we praise and worship, we are bringing John to the Lord and into the center of the Lord's presence and to what He wants to do for John. It's in this atmosphere of praise and worship that the Lord's ear is inclined to hear and He releases His anointing. At the same time John's spirit is being touched even if he himself is unable to pray or seemingly respond outwardly. Exactly the same principle applies if we are praying for a person at a distance who isn't with us.

The demonic powers hate our praise and worship. They hear and know when our hearts are truly turning to God for His help. We put them to flight when we come into this place. It's not praise and worship out of habit but out of a heart turned towards the Lord with a true hunger for His presence.

Singing praise and worship hymns and songs is a powerful way of ushering in the presence of the Lord. We were once praying with a person who had come out from a satanic cult and we were helping her respond to the Lord in worship. As we began to sing a song called, *'We place you in the highest place, for you are our great High Priest'*, a smug look came over the person's face.

It turned out that the demonic powers were happy with this song and gladly joined in with agreement. We quickly realized that the demonic beings were agreeing with the words but applying them to their deity! As soon as we added in the name of Jesus, the smug look disappeared and instead the person battled to say the words until victory came.

We learnt an important lesson that our worship songs need to have the name of Jesus within them. Otherwise the 'other side' can take the words and receive the worship. On another occasion with the same person we sang the hymn *'O Jesus I have promised to serve thee to the end'*. The demonic powers within her became enraged. They hated this expression of covenant and tried all manner of tricks to keep the person from singing. As the lady persevered and pushed through, she received a powerful deliverance.

The prayer of cleansing

As part of our worship and praise, our hearts need cleansing.

> *Have mercy on me, O God, according to your steadfast love; according to your abundant mercy blot out my transgressions. Wash me thoroughly from my iniquity, and cleanse me from my sin... You desire truth in the inward being; therefore teach me wisdom in my secret heart.*
>
> *Purge me with hyssop, and I shall be clean; wash me, and I shall be whiter than snow.*
>
> Psalm 51:1-2 & 6-7

Part of worship and preparation for healing is bringing our hearts before the Lord for cleansing. As fallen mankind, we all need to bring our hearts before God so that His Holy Spirit can show us things which need confessing.

Our prayer needs to be along the lines of, "Lord we ask you to cleanse our hearts and to give us the right motivation for coming before you today. We give you permission to show us things which we need to put right."

In modeling this prayer and saying it sincerely for ourselves, it releases the person we are helping to also open up their heart to God.

The prayer of consecration

Over the years of praying with individuals, we have learnt the power in consecration. The enemy knows when something is dedicated and consecrated to God. Of course the danger in all of these things is that we can get things out of balance and become superstitious as a result. However, that's not enough reason to throw the baby out with the bathwater and to ignore the reality, which is that consecration matters to God and the demonic powers are disempowered as a result.

The bible talks of an inward consecration; *'Therefore, my friends, since we have confidence to enter the sanctuary by the blood of Jesus, by the new and living way that he opened for us through the curtain (that is through his flesh), and since we have a great priest over the house of God, let us approach with a true heart in full assurance of faith, with our hearts sprinkled clean from an evil conscience and our bodies washed with pure water. Let us hold fast to the confession of our hope without wavering for he who has promised is faithful'*, Hebrews 10:19-23.

When we speak aloud our consecration to the Lord, it's a powerful declaration which the powers of darkness take note of. We are clearly on the Lord's side and if they attack us, then they take on a battle which will eventually mean they lose their ground. God will turn around their attacks to plunder Satan's kingdom and give us victory in the battle.

So I like to pray in this way; "Lord, we consecrate ourselves to You for Your purposes this day and we dedicate Judy to you and ask You to consecrate her and to set her apart for You to do Your work within her." This will help to release the anointing of the Lord.

There is also the consecration of the places where we are ministering.

Then you shall take the anointing oil, and anoint the tabernacle and all that is in it, and consecrate it and all its furniture, so that it shall become holy.

Exodus 40:9

I have heard your prayer and your plea, which you made before me; I have consecrated this house that you have built, and put my name there forever, my eyes and my heart will be there for all time.

1 Kings 9:3

The Lord sees and knows what is consecrated to Him and set apart for His purpose and for His glory. The powers of darkness also see and take note and they flee when they see God's people taking seriously the Word of the Lord and acting upon it.

There have been many hundreds of times when we have experienced breakthroughs in prayer following consecration and dedication. Obviously church buildings have usually been consecrated and dedicated. However, I don't believe this is an act which must only be done once and for all. Over years of use, buildings become defiled through the sin of the leaders or of those using and entering the buildings. A building may also have become defiled by objects placed there. Neither can we ever know if there has been some deliberate cursing of a building.

The enemy of souls doesn't just give up and go away because a building is consecrated. In fact it's usually just the opposite. The enemy wants to steal what belongs to God, so if he can invade and occupy a church building through rights given by sinful acts and agreements, he will do so. Having gained such access, he will do the work of bringing division and spiritual death. This is why it is so necessary that the gift of discernment is exercised and used against the powers of darkness concerning buildings and objects.

There will be many occasions when we aren't ministering or praying on consecrated ground and even if it is consecrated, this consecration may need re-enforcing if we are unsure what may have taken place in that place. Ministering in hospitals, homes, schools, conference venues or in the outdoors are some examples.

We have held some of our conferences in public settings. I remember the time when the previous usage for the venue was a rock concert. The center had been contaminated physically as well as spiritual. The staff of this area were very distressed at the state of the building and most apologetic.

As a team, we knew our work was to do both spiritual and physical cleansing.

We applied the principles we have learnt about cleansing land, buildings and objects. We had legal rights to be in the center for an allotted period, for we had rented it. Therefore we had rights to dedicate and consecrate it for holy purposes during our time there.

We prayed and asked the Lord to send His angels to help us and we took authority over powers of darkness that would disrupt the meeting, oppress the people or hamper the anointing. We prayed over some oil and anointed the doors, floors and windows. The spiritual atmosphere tangibly lifted and we were able to have a holy and precious time of praise and worship and ministry unhindered in any way spiritually.

There will be times when all of us spend times of prayer within a building which is used for all sorts of purposes and the buildings themselves will have become spiritually oppressed by the events which have taken place within. For example hospitals will certainly be affected by the consequences of trauma, infirmity and death. A building used for business may be defiled by such things as dishonesty, blasphemy, or crudeness.

We can ask the Lord to come by His Holy Spirit and cleanse the room, specifically mentioning things which are likely to have affected it. We can consecrate the room to be used for holy purposes during the time we are occupying it.

Praying and asking the Lord to consecrate and dedicate a particular room when we are about to minister to an individual or to hold an important spiritual meeting will release an anointing for the purpose and aid us in our work and purpose. It will bring the Lord's presence and repel darkness. We want to experience heaven coming to earth.

The prayer of declaration

But they have conquered him (the accuser) by the blood of the Lamb and by the word of their testimony.

Revelation 12:11

Part of our worship and relationship with God is to proclaim out loud the truth which is in our hearts. The outward confessing with our lips of an inward truth is powerful in the spirit realm.

When ministering to people, I encourage them to speak out their conviction of who God is, what He has done and what they are believing for. I believe that it's important that our spirits are empowered and energized. Our 'soulish' state will seek to trap us into a complacent place. It is when we speak something out with our lips that the battle will begin.

Satan hates declaration and testimony. The power of the spoken word going forth is a weapon, with which we overcome his power in our lives. When we speak out, we own what we say and it becomes reinforced and part of us. It begins to shake those doubts which grow when something is kept on the inside. The agreement we make with God in our testifying releases strength and power to our inner being. The conviction of truth puts the enemy into fear and he flees.

We can declare: "Lord Jesus, I belong to You. Jesus is Lord here. The plans of the Lord Jesus Christ will go forth in my life. We declare our trust in Jesus today. Jesus is healing and trans-forming me".

The prayer of agreement

"If in my name you ask me for anything, I will do it."

John 14:14

Truly I tell you, whatever you bind on earth will be bound in heaven and whatever you loose on earth will be loosed in heaven. Again, truly I tell you, if two of you agree on earth about anything you ask, it will be done for you by my Father in heaven. For where two or three are gathered in my name, I am there among them.

Matthew 18:18-20

There are two kinds of agreement we can make. Both of these have a powerful effect in our praying. The first kind is our personal agreement with God and the second is when we agree with others and God.

In the first instance, when we personally align our free will with God's will, there's a spiritual transaction between God and man which can't be broken. This is why it's so imperative that we help people to come in submission to God and to agree with His ways and His truth for their lives. No amount of our doing this in our lives or saying the words for them will have any effect. God needs every person's free will joined to His will.

The prayer of agreement goes hand in hand with the prayer of declaration, for it's in the prayer of declaration that powerful agreements are made with God. Yes, the enemy will surely come and challenge it. He will try and break our agreements. His purpose is to try and tempt us into agreeing with him! If he can, he will have us say things like "God doesn't love me", "I am a useless failure", "there's no hope for me", "I would be better off forgetting this God stuff" or even worse "I would be better off dead than like this".

Satan likes to work on our feelings. The problem is that our feelings feel to us as though they are the truth! However, feelings can lead us down the garden path. They can deceive us. Yes, they feel like they are truth. They are real and it hurts. However, God wants to bring our feelings into line with His truth. In order to do this, He needs our agreement as to what *is* truth. Jesus said in John 14:6, *"I am the Way, the Truth and the Life. No man comes to the Father but by Me."*

What is the truth really? The truth from the bible is that I'm loved by God - He is changing me, I'm not useless, I'm not beyond help, and I'm going to live and declare the glorious deeds of the Lord. There are many ways we can bring people into powerful freedom by identifying where they have allowed the enemy access through ungodly agreements.

Then there are the agreements made between us as individuals with God. Often we don't realize how very powerful these can be for the release of God's power. However, it must be said that the opposite is also true. We probably don't realize how much the power of agreement can be snatched by the enemy to bring death and destruction either to ourselves or to others. Our words and agreements hold great power for good and evil: Proverbs 18:21.

Agreements we make together can be snatched by the enemy and used in the spiritual realm as curses if they hold a malicious intent. However, they can also be used in the spiritual realm to release the power of 'soulishness' which we will look at in another chapter.

The biblical principle of binding and loosing is an interesting one for the intercessory role (Matthew 18:18). In our binding the power of the enemy, we loose (release) the power of God here on the earth. We can also loose the captive here on earth and they will be given release (loosing) in heaven. When we speak out that we release and free an individual into their gifting, destiny and calling there's an effect in the heavenly realm which can aid that release. The Lord is looking for our unity (agreement) of purpose.

One and one doesn't make two with the Lord! He works with divine multiplication. So when we make heartfelt and sincere agreements in line with God's plan and purpose, it will surely come to pass here on earth. Timing may be something we have to learn but nevertheless God doesn't forget His promises.

The prayer of covenant

In 2 Samuel 23:5, David says, *"Is not my house like this with God? For he has made with me an everlasting covenant, ordered in all things and secure. Will he not cause to prosper all my help and my desire?"*

God desires that we remind Him of His covenant and His promises with us as His children. He hears our words and our cries. They move His heart to action. If we sit back and do nothing, believing God will do what He will do, we may never see all that God intended for us as individuals or in the corporate sense. Our participation is invited and without it, there is no meaningful relationship.

The covenant God has with His people is the highest form of relationship. God's covenant can't be broken. We can run away from God but He will never move away from us. Satan will seek to use his ways bringing torment, shame, guilt, defilement and the perpetration of evil in an attempt to divide and separate us from our loving God. He will use these things to cause us to believe in his lies and accusations and in order to steal the worship which belongs to God.

Scripture describes Satan as a thief and a robber. This is his nature and character and it hasn't changed since the day he fell out of the heavenly realms because he wanted the worship which belongs to God. In our intercession for others we must help them to remind God of His promises and to put their trust in a covenant-keeping God. Identifying the work of the thief and the robber will be a vital part of this.

I pray something like this: "Lord You are our covenant-keeping God and we are here today as Your children relying on Your promises. We declare a higher court here today than any other court and in this place of authority we ask You to break all ungodly agreements, promises, oaths, pacts, vows and rituals which the enemy would hold against Judy. We agree together for Judy's freedom and that the enemy is under our feet."

It is from this place that we can begin the work of bringing healing and restoration. We will have given the powers of darkness notice that they are being exposed and we are also appropriating the promises of God and the inheritance He has won for us.

God's Covenant

Unless we understand that our Heavenly Father is a covenantal God, we will be severely restricted in our ability to access and move into His plans for us and others with true faith and assurance.

Love is a small word which sums up the nature and character of God (1 John 4:8). It is not that God made a decision to love. If this was so then it would mean that God could equally well decide to stop being love. God IS love, it is His inescapable personhood, nature and character. God can't remove Himself from who He is as a loving God.

The same is true with covenant. The covenant is not a set of promises God decided to give to the human race. The covenant is who God *is*, His nature and character. In the Hebrew language the word 'hesed' means covenant. When it is found in the Old Testament, the word 'hesed' or covenant, is often translated into English as (God's) loving-kindness, mercy, tenderness or faithfulness. We have a God who is faithful, who is merciful and full of loving-kindness, just and true.

God's love is not an emotion which comes and goes. Rather, it is like a multi-faceted diamond which encompasses the breadth, the width, height and depth of the very nature of the Godhead (Father, Son and Holy Spirit). As such, it is something we can stand on and place our complete trust in because God's love is true and real.

The bible tells us that '*in Him we live and move and have our being*' (Acts 17:28) and in Colossians 1:17, '*through Him all things hold together.*' We have our existence and are held together by the love of God and His covenant. This is true for every member of the human race. God created us in His love and His desire is for each of us to have relationship with Him through Jesus His Son.

God initiates relationship with us by covenant, not by contract. He doesn't give us a set of rules to adhere to. He gives us His promises and guarantee as to how safe and secure our 'sonship' and our inheritance is with Him. ('Sonship' is a term which applies equally to the female part of the body of Christ.) Jesus became our representative before the Father. He became our guarantor. In His willing death, He stood in our place and guaranteed for us our position as sons, daughters and heirs with Him.

Jesus went before us as our intercessor, standing in the gap on our behalf, so that we may freely receive forgiveness and mercy. We may enter into all that our Father longs for us to have as His children. We can therefore enter boldly on the grounds of covenant and be sure and certain that we are accepted and embraced.

It is from this place of utter security and safety that we can begin to learn and grow in our relationship with God. In order to grow and learn healthily, a child will have to make mistakes. It's an essential part of learning and growing. Our covenantal God knows this is true in our relationship with Him, and as a loving Father He teaches us, helps us and places us in safety.

If we think we must earn God's love or obey rules to appease God and therefore win His love, we have completely missed the point of covenant. We will pray according to contract rather than according to covenant. This will affect our ability to pray effectively, to break through into the victory which is ours in Christ, either for ourselves or others.

Substituting contract for covenant

I have prayed with many people who approach God on the terms of contract rather than covenant. Some have never had teaching on covenant and the faithfulness of God. Others have great difficulty in believing God is love or that He is faithful and they approach Him with a human fear rather than awe at the majesty, beauty and holiness of God. This kind of awe gives us a holy fear of God rather than the kind of fear which makes us timid, afraid, insecure and lacking in confidence.

An unhealthy approach to God will oppose faith and trust. A healthy approach to God, on the other hand, will produce boldness and tenacity. We will look at the subject of faith in the next chapter.

Contract means that we obey terms and conditions and have to pay for what we get. We somehow have to work it out and get it right. Contract means that we will hesitate to enter into that which has been already been bought for us! We may be apologetic and try to clean ourselves up before we come to God our Father in Heaven. Yet Jesus has freely opened up the way for us to enter in and receive our inheritance.

The miracle of the incarnation is that Jesus came down from heaven into the mess of this world and into the mess of our lives. He didn't expect us to climb out of our mess, clean ourselves up and get our lives together before He accepted us! Our Heavenly Father saw how much we needed Him. We are fallen human beings who without divine intervention are incapable of being clean and sinless.

We have a God of love who in His covenantal nature came to earth and rescued us from ourselves and placed us with Him in heavenly places. He calls us His 'sons' and He gives us His inheritance on the grounds of covenant. He has bought us by His precious blood and the stamp of His ownership is upon us (Ephesians 1:13). His desire is that we turn to Him in childlike trust and faith, acknowledging that we need Him to forgive us, cleanse us, renew us and empower us within by His Holy Spirit.

It's from this place that our prayers will become increasingly effective and powerful. We will grow and learn more confidently how faithful God is and how He keeps His promises.

This is *not* to say that we can be presumptuous in prayer, as though God is going to give us everything we ask for and demand.

Small children growing up need to learn that they are not the center of the universe, nor are they going to have all their demands met. Children have to learn consideration and care for others and to fit in accordingly.

At the same time however, it's right that children learn that they are precious and valuable and that they are heard and understood. As a team we have prayed with countless people who remain damaged in adulthood because as children they were overridden by the expectations of their parents to the extent that their own personhood and spirit was deeply crushed.

It's no wonder that such people have enormous difficulty in approaching God's throne with any confidence or expectation of an answer. They may hold deep 'core' beliefs that God has no time for them, that they're in the way, that He's angry with them or that He's ashamed of them.

Demanding answers from God

It is true that other people, when praying, appear to think they have a divine right to demand answers from God, and that His answers must come in their way. Consequently when difficulties come, they become disheartened and even disillusioned by struggle and suffering. For them, it's as though God is not who He says He is – a faithful, loving and secure God. They find the greatest difficulty in trusting God.

When I have counseled such people, I see the roots of independence which have come from a painful past. I understand why they have decided to take matters into their own hands. The fear of rejection, of being let down, of domination and sometimes deep betrayal have led them to become their own authority to one degree or another and so it's hard for them to trust God to lead and guide them. Their deep-seated lack of trust means they don't fully yield themselves to God. Their need to control leads them to try (subconsciously) to control God.

Many of these roots come from mother or father issues. Submission and authority issues and pain are transferred onto God.

Hidden inner beliefs are alive on the inside and cause blockages
and hindrances in their relationship with God. This is one reason
why the healing ministry is needed for a healthy and mature walk
with the Lord. These roots can be identified and brought to God
for inner transformation and freedom.

We can then gain the victory over the enemy who loves to work
in these hidden areas of our life and pull the strings of pain, fear,
mistrust, domination, injustice, anger, abandonment and rejection.
From these unhealed areas many sinful attitudes spring up and then
consequential behaviors which reinforce our opinion of how shame-
ful, sinful and bad we are. From this place, the enemy condemns us
and enjoys our seeming lack of victory and sense of failure.

Praise the Lord, there are answers for the injustice we may have
received and there's freedom in the name of Jesus which has been
won and assured for us. Many Ellel Ministries' courses and books
offer practical and spiritual help for those areas of our lives where
we may be struggling or where we simply need to receive truth and
light. The Word of God is living and active (Hebrews 4:12). It's not
a dead book but a living book which is full of practical application.

A question we need to ask is whether there are any conditions
for covenant. Scripture speaks powerfully of the blessings of being
in covenant and these are especially outlined in the Old Testament
in Deuteronomy 28. But in then the New Testament, Jesus speaks
of covenant relationship when He says, "If you love me, you will
obey me" (John 14:21).

God's covenantal relationship with us doesn't change, so in that
respect it's completely unconditional. However, if we choose to
walk away from the blessings of living in covenant under divine
protection and within the boundaries God lays down for us, like
the prodigal son, we will suffer.

When we hold onto our way of self protection and living life
our way and we disregard and disobey God's best way for us, then
He will allow us to reap what we sow (Galatians 6:7). He simply
waits for us to come back to Him in fresh trust. God does not com-
pete for a place in our lives and He will patiently wait for us to
return to Him in rightful sorrow of heart (repentance) and fresh

trust in Him. If we don't do this and we go on to cause ourselves
and others great damage, He will be filled with pain and grief but
He won't override our free will.

Learning to trust God

Our place of intercession needs to be from a place where we reach
out in yielded childlike faith and trust to our loving and covenantal
God. He will then move in our lives and in the lives of those we
pray for in His way not *our* way. It may not be the way we would
choose or want but it will be the *best* way.

We may not immediately be able to see this, but as we trust God
there will be a time when we *will* be able to see the infinite wisdom
of God and be full of gratitude to Him. We will grow in our confidence in God and in our trust in His ways. We will start to see that
He is working out His eternal purposes through us.

Twenty years ago, when I began to pray for people, I used to
sweat and shake with the responsibility. I was so nervous my knees
would sometimes knock! God was very merciful to me because
in my weakness He helped me grow and learn. Today I am much
more confident. This confidence is not confidence in my ability
but I have truly learnt to be confident in Him.

If at the end of a meeting someone comes up to me and says,
"the Lord really touched me through what you said today" and I
know they are saying it from deep in their heart, it fills me with
joy. I'm not so concerned about whether I, as a human being, was
performing well. My fulfillment and joy is in how the Lord has
used me to reach others. It is in this I have confidence.

So it is with our prayers. God wants us to be confident in what
He can and will do through each of us as human, fallible vessels
who are walking in relationship with our covenant keeping God.

Oaths and pacts

I have included this section to help any of you who may be praying for those who are suffering and struggling with issues of free

will and where the enemy may have gained access through their involvement in the occult or religions where oaths and pacts have been made, either by someone on their behalf or by themselves

The enemy of God knows the ground on which we stand when we pray. If he has rights in our lives, he won't just give up and walk away. Satan is the god of contract. When we have areas in our lives that have given him rights, he will use them.

When promises, dedications, rituals, oaths, pacts or baptisms are made to false gods or more powerfully directly in the name of Satan, there will be curses attached to them.

These curses need to be identified and broken in the name of Jesus Christ and freedom entered into through the covenant blessing of all Jesus won for us. He took on Himself our guilt and broke the curse (Galatians 3:13).

This is why we must pray from a place of covenant. We have prayed for countless people who have come under great oppression, sickness and spiritual darkness through the outworking of various oaths and pacts made in the past. The enemy contends highly in these areas and at times we have witnessed severe battles as a result.

During those battles, it has seemed that the person we have prayed for has been rendered helpless and under a control outside of themselves. The way to freedom has come when we have helped people understand that this isn't a battle between opposing forces which are equal - for God and Satan aren't equal. Also they themselves aren't to be passive victims.

Satan is a legalist. A person I know once described Satan as the world's foremost legal expert who charges the highest rates! As a legalist, he contends on the grounds of contract and in his court of law. But our position is outside his court of law and in the highest court of all – the court of Jesus Christ seated in the heavenly realms, with Him as Judge.

Jesus is the highest judge of all. *He* delivers the verdict over us and it's based on covenant. When Jesus died on the cross, He cried *'it is finished* (John 19:30). It's on this basis and in this court of covenant that we have the authority to undo all the work of the evil one.

However the people concerned have to enter into their covenant blessing. They have to trust the Lord to reveal hidden darkness and then to deal with words, actions, pacts, oaths and rituals that have been entered into through a contract with the enemy, even if those have been done unwittingly in ignorance or they've been done by others on their behalf. Of course those which have been entered into willingly will be powerful and will need thorough repentance, renunciation and deliverance.

I remember once praying with a lady who had been high up in the occult and the powers of darkness were contending for her life. We all agreed to sing the famous hymn, 'O Jesus I have promised to serve you to the end' and in another verse of the same hymn the words say, 'O Jesus you have promised to all who follow you, that where you are in glory there shall your servant be.' The demonic powers within her absolutely raged at these words and she experienced a powerful deliverance.

Our grounds are on the sure and certain promises of God to us, revealed in Scripture and this is the solid ground.

Reaching out for God's will

In any given situation, there may be many ways in which God wants to reveal His will for us. I have found that many people become muddled in this area of finding God's will. They can often become very bound, fretful and confused, believing that God has not heard them or that they must have got something very wrong.

God's will is inextricably bound to our will! This may be news to you, but it's because God has bound Himself to us in covenantal love and He can't withdraw this. What we do with our will and choices affects Him.

Even if we choose to go into the worst kind of rebellion or sin, God doesn't remove Himself from us. It will grieve Him and bring about a loss of protection for us, as we go out of our boundary of safety, but it will never stop God loving us and being bound to us in covenant-keeping promises.

This is how it is in any family where a teenage child refuses to listen or trust the wisdom of a parent and deliberately chooses to rebel and enter into things which are dangerous and wrong. The parent can't stop the teenager if they are intent on their quest for rebellion but neither can the teenager stop the parent from praying, loving and believing for a turnaround. Even if the teenager doesn't turn around for many years, the parental love is not withdrawn.

So, it is with God. His love and covenantal relationship are there for us even in our deepest rebellion. We have the story of the Prodigal Son in Luke 5. This gives us full assurance of the heart of God. The father in the story put the best robes on his son and a ring on his finger when he returned home in repentance. Punishment or blame was far from the father's heart because the father was primarily overcome with joy that his son had returned home with a repentant and humble heart.

When we do walk with the Lord in His covenantal love, and we have a decision to make, He wants us to be free to look at the many choices and options there are. He desires that we should be free to find out about ourselves, our gifting, our talent, our individual and unique personhood and our circumstances, all of which combine to help us make a balanced choice and decision.

God has set us in relationships and given us family, friends and those in authority over us in whom He asks us to trust, in order to receive input, correction and direction. God is not a dictator and He did *not* make us robots. God is a relational God and His desire is for relationship with us. Our free will and choice is *precious* to Him. In His wisdom, He gives us an array of factors which help us to make our decisions.

God also gives us boundaries which are safe. Protected by these we can grow and develop. In the course of our lives, desiring God's way and purposes, we may go down many avenues. God will always use these avenues even if they seem to be mistakes or they ended up causing pain. Even if we were not desiring God's ways, His covenant promises are to *redeem the years the locusts have eaten* (Joel 2:25). Nothing is ever lost to Him that He can't and won't bring into His redemption and higher purposes if we allow Him to.

When praying for God's will in our lives or for others, God desires that we simply approach Him on the basis of trust. Our humanity sometimes wants everything to be simplified, in a black and white category with no blurred edges. In fact, if we were honest, we would like an audible blast from heaven on occasions!

However, these things are rare. Mostly, God speaks with us and leads us through life's experiences and circumstances. We have a God full of wisdom (Proverbs 2:6). Asking the Lord for His wisdom and counsel is the way for us to receive ideas, thoughts and prayers which otherwise wouldn't have entered our minds. We all need the mind of Christ (1 Corinthians 2:16) and to be filled with the knowledge of God (Ephesians 4:13).

God also gives us the inner witness and power of His Holy Spirit to help guide and lead us. Remember it's God's heart to strengthen, help and guide us (Psalm 50:15 and Psalm 25:4-14).

Using the tools and principles of His kingdom will help us to engage in prayer and intercession which brings heaven down to earth. Many of these are outlined in this book. However, we need to remember these are not magic. They aren't techniques. Our growing relationship with the Lord is the essence of praying powerfully. It's on the grounds of covenant - which moves the heart of God to hear and answer, guide and lead us.

God wants us to remind Him of His promises (Psalm 119:49 and Isaiah 62:6). In our relationship with Him, He likes to hear us using His Word which is full of His covenantal promises to us. In doing so, this strengthens us and causes belief and faith to be unleashed and to rise up. Our spirit comes alive in a fresh way and meets with God's Spirit which is reaching out to us. Something takes place in the heavenly realms – a power of agreement between us and God.

When faith and trust are strengthened within us, it leads us to a releasing place where we watch how God will work out His will and purposes in and through any given situation. His ways are *far above our ways and His thoughts are higher than our thoughts*' (Isaiah 55:8-9).

Prayer of Faith and Breakthrough

We know we need faith to pray effectively. But faith is a complex word, so in this chapter we will look at some of its aspects. For how can we pray without faith? As I outlined in the last chapter, faith must arise out of relationship. Faith can't be exercised like a piece of magic or a technique. God is looking for those who are reaching out to Him from a place of childlike trust. It's from this place in our relationship with Him that we will begin to see mountains and obstacles moved.

However, all of us can be ignorant about the ways of God, and this can hold us back in our walk of faith and trust. There's no condemnation in this because we are all learners and on our own personal journey of discovery, both about ourselves and about God. Sometimes, it's not so much what we need to learn about God as what we need to learn about ourselves. I believe this is the most common reason why exercising faith is difficult. The problems are rooted in our relationship with God and we will look at this area later on in the chapter.

Faith is a small word which encompasses so much. Our aspirations, our dreams, our needs, the desperate situations, the seemingly impossible, they all come into the way we desire to pray with faith.

Sometimes, we try to muster up faith. We feel we *should* have faith for something we know to be God's will and yet find there is none. Sometimes we've prayed for something so much and so many times, we have lost hope or belief. At other times, we have given up praying; believing God has not heard or is not answering. Some may have faced situations in life which need a miracle, and without that miracle they are faced with the sheer impossibility of carrying on.

Diseases, sicknesses, handicap, dire financial needs, relational impossibilities and many other issues of injustice come into this category. Where is God in the place of suffering and impossibility and how do we pray with faith?

My husband Peter was trained as a scientist in chemistry. He has often told me that it's easier to have faith in something once we understand it. For example, we have faith to sit on a chair when we can see it's solid, has four legs and is on the ground! We have faith it will stay on the ground because we know that gravity holds it there and so we can put the weight of our whole being on it.

From this illustration, we learn that faith is easier to apply with some knowledge. I have certainly learnt this from my experience in the healing ministry. As I have understood God's principles for healing, deliverance and discipleship and applied them, I have seen transformation and radical changes in people's lives. My faith has grown by leaps and bounds as a result.

For example, I once prayed with someone who was imprisoned for something he didn't do. Another person had wrongly accused him and it led to imprisonment with the consequential loss of their reputation, livelihood, relationships and personal freedom. You could say this person had a *right* to be bitter. However, this bitterness ate him up to the point where his whole body was physically very sick. His body was reflecting the sickness of his soul and spirit.

In time and with the tender love of God being brought into his life he was enabled to fully release and forgive the perpetrators. We went on to witness a miraculous physical healing - and also a powerful inner transformation. We could see that he was set free to walk into God's redemptive purposes and without the shackles of injustice and bitterness. This experience gave me increased faith to pray with others for physical healing where areas of bitterness were identified.

I have been privileged to witness miracles of healing. These miracles haven't come whenever I would have liked them to, but nevertheless, the fact that I have seen what God can do in the face of impossibility has increased my faith. I can trust in Him as an all-knowing and faithful God. I believe He's utterly trustworthy with our lives.

As marvelous and wonderful as it is to see miracles and to witness God moving powerfully in people's lives, we do need to consider those Christians who are suffering and struggling with what seems to be impossible situations.

Faith for the daily walk

It's important to look at both sides of the coin. Both kinds of a walk of faith are valid for us as Christians and both have equally deep dimensions. They aren't opposed to one another. Our Christian faith is full of what are seemingly contradictory truths such as 'God's love is unconditional' but also 'God's love has conditions'. The gift of God's love can't be looked at just as an intellectual fact. It's a gift we are required to take, open and use.

We need the spiritual gift of faith to believe for the impossible. We need the application of faith to unpack the components and to see the God of the impossible work a miracle.

But faith isn't just needed where there are impossibilities. Faith is a necessary part of our walk with God each day. We will be unable to move into greater realms of faith unless we have lived the faith walk in areas of life that are less testing but are still just as much needed.

The bible tells us it is impossible to please God without faith (Hebrews 11:6). It may be easier for us to understand the word 'faith' by describing it as trust. Placing our whole trust into the hands of God our Father releases the heart of God to hear and answer our prayer. It pleases Him that, as His created ones, we have faith and trust in Him as our Creator.

One of the problems for us as created beings is that our knowledge holds itself up against the knowledge of God. We think we know better. We believe we can fix the problems, difficulties and impossibilities. In fact, if man was left to his own way, he would try to be God. Our pride stands in opposition to God (1 Peter 4:5-6).

The reality is that our triune God (Father, Son and Holy Spirit) has created us and has given us limitations here on earth as to how much we can and can't do. All our knowledge comes from God but if we use that knowledge to go out of 'created order' then man will find that, rather than knowledge being a blessing, it will bring cursing.

This side of eternity we live with limitations of energy, time and resource. We aren't granted a limitless supply. Due to original sin and this world's fallen state, where there is death and decay, we can't go beyond the limits that God sets. It's within this context that we can apply our faith.

For instance, it would be stupidity to apply faith to believe that someone will suddenly become ten years younger than they are! Faith has to be based on some reality, even though the bible tells us that faith for something we can already see is not faith at all!

The key is balance. We need God's wisdom to apply our faith prayer in a balanced and real way, without that balance becoming an easy excuse for us to doubt that God will change the situation we are asking Him to change.

Faith where the outcome is life or death

My experience with faith is that God sometimes requires us to hold equal and opposite tensions. So, for instance we may have a loved one who has been given a diagnosis of cancer which is terminal. We may have been told they don't have long to live. It is absolutely natural for us all as Christians to want to pray with faith that God will heal and restore.

We may pray all we know how to pray and ask many others to do likewise. Yet, we are quite likely to still see the progression of the disease and, for some of us, we have gone on to witness our loved ones die. We may well ask what happened to all that faith. We may have been sure that God would heal and have been left with disappointment and pain in our heart towards God.

I have witnessed a few of my friends and family in this situation. I used to think that perhaps I didn't have enough faith or maybe I just didn't pray the right prayer or pray hard enough. However, as the years have gone by the Lord has demonstrated to me that my faith is not being misplaced, nor has He withheld His healing or love.

God responds to faith in different ways. We need faith to believe He's with us and as we assure others that God is present, there's a release of anointing and power. We also need faith to believe that God will sustain a person in suffering. As we apply our trust in God in our prayer for this, He releases His anointing to do the things we ask.

When we bind and break the power of the enemy in someone's life and take up our authority in Jesus' name, we are applying faith. Again God's anointing is released and the need we are praying for is met. There are many tools and weapons of the kingdom of God which need our faith for their successful application and then we see the fulfillment of God's covenant promises.

It is very easy when we see someone decline, to take it on board that our prayers are not being answered. We need faith to remember that God is working His purposes out His way. For example, there have been times when I knew that God was not going to heal the disease of cancer for the person I was praying with. I had no inner certainty or witness that He would heal. However, neither did I want to stand in the way of God bringing about a miracle.

God is Sovereign and the mystery is that He does sometimes intervene in the affairs of men against all odds. Nothing is too difficult for Him. It's not for us to dictate how or when He should do this, but the mystery is that our prayers and faith do change things. What I have done in these situations is ask the Lord to miraculously heal, but at the same time I tell Him that even if He doesn't, I'm still trusting Him with everything concerning my loved one.

It's from this position of trust and faith, I have seen God do marvelous things in the suffering person's life. He draws intimately close to them and reveals much to them. There is a quality and beauty even in their suffering. God has held bound the powers of darkness which have sought to torment, confuse and control the sufferer.

The Lord has released a powerful anointing for life in the midst of the process of disease and death and has taken the loved one home to be with Himself at exactly the right time and in complete peace. So, we see that faith for a miracle is not the only application of faith in impossible situations. Our allowing God to be God and our holding both equal positions of faith in tension is not wrong or lacking in faith.

We have to be careful that the natural man's fear of dying and death don't stand in the way of the release God wants to bring. There's no sting in death for the Christian even if there's grief here on earth for those left behind. For the Christian, we don't die but pass away from this earth's reality and from our earthly body into our heavenly reality and eventually our heavenly body. This is a glorious transition which needs to be filled with faith!

We are designed by God to live life, hold onto life and enjoy His gift of life. It would be unnatural for any one of us to want our loved one to die but if the evidence is there that God is taking them home, it will take faith to trust Him to do so, and in His time. What faith!

God has placed eternity in our hearts and our time here on earth is but a minute part of the whole of eternity. Even in a tragic death or premature death, nothing is lost to God and therefore to us. From the perspective of eternity, God is holding our loved ones in His safe keeping and His eternal purposes for a time ahead which will hold limitless joy when we are reunited. Our grief for our loss during our time here on earth is what we will need to work through.

Our intercessory role is to help those facing or living with tragic circumstances here on earth, to live in and experience the eternal dimension of faith. This can't be spoken out with words alone, they are imparted through the faith and certainty in our hearts as intercessors.

Faith to live in difficult and painful circumstances

It also takes great faith to live in conditions which are difficult, painful and cause suffering. God is pleased with this kind of deep and real faith. In this place He will respond by strengthening us, giving us grace and a peace beyond that which is humanly possible. It is well said that when we come to the end of our human resource, God steps in with His resources. Our prayers in and from this place are very powerful.

This is the prayer God loves to hear and answer. It pleases Him because we have come to an end of ourselves and have placed ourselves utterly in His hands. It is the kind of prayer people cry when accidents are about to occur. Nothing can be done except by divine intervention.

Faith where only God can intervene

We had a situation within the life of Ellel Ministries when we prayed the prayer of desperation. There have been many times when we have been up against it financially and needed a breakthrough. God has been so gracious to us and answered prayer in different ways and we are still alive to tell the tale!

However, many years ago, there was one time when we were in severe difficulty. In fact the bank was at the end of what they were able to do for us and time had run out on our ability to pay our bills. One of our leaders spoke to the team at our morning prayer time and told them that this was like a time of being under siege where there was nowhere to go and nothing could be done. He exhorted the team to stand firm and not to move from their posts, we would trust the Lord for a breakthrough. As leaders, we could not fix it; it had to be God's intervention.

Our leader had released faith and hope into the team. Again it shows that when we speak out and declare a faith position and put ourselves on the line, God honors this. On that particular day, it was wonderful to tangibly feel the sense of peace and faith that surrounded the team as the Lord brought His anointing.

However, this did nothing to change the circumstances immediately and we were still left in dire straights. Our executive leadership had a meeting, and we were left with no illusions. The prayer
of desperation was all we could pray and we cried out to God,
"God this is your work, unless you save it and provide for it, there's
nothing more we can do. Please help us Lord." Peace came and
there was nothing for it but to continue with the ordinary business
and place our faith and trust in God.

A couple of days later, my husband Peter had a sense that he
should ring David Cross who was the leader of Glyndley Manor.
It was beyond midnight and I remember thinking this was very
late to be ringing someone. Peter persisted and it was a definite
nudging from the Lord to do so. David told Peter he had just been
sorting out a potentially very dangerous situation.

Some men in balaclavas with truncheons in their hands had
broken into Glyndley Manor on this particular evening. Mercifully
most of the team were out. However, there was a new member of
the young people's team in the building and also a lady who had
come for ministry. The armed men demanded to know where the
safe was kept. Obviously they were after money.

The young person was Polish and couldn't answer as she didn't
speak much English and didn't understand what was being said!
The lady who had come for help was so full of joy from her day's
ministry that she was confident enough to tell the men that she
was a visitor and didn't know anything!

These very angry men found the room nearby where the safe
was kept. They couldn't undo it and in frustration they left the
building. No-one was harmed and nothing taken, even though
there was nothing there anyway! God had allowed the men to
enter but He didn't allow them to do any damage. As Peter and
David spoke on the phone they both gave thanks to the Lord for
His incredible protection and safeguarding of us. They both realized that the Lord would allow the enemy to go so far, even to create a rumpus on occasions, but no further.

It was the following day that we had the *breakthrough* on our
finances. There was a phone call to our accountant from an

unknown person who had once prayed that if they had £100,000, they would give it to Ellel Ministries. God had heard this person's prayer of sincerity and faith. In an incredible way, this person subsequently came into a surprise inheritance which was not an inheritance from their own family.

They were obedient to their word and to their promise to God. They rang us to say that the check would be coming for the full amount they had promised God. The timing of this could not have been more perfect for our needs.

We have no doubt whatsoever that great reward is stored up for this person in heaven. They were not a person with personal means or riches. They gave out of simple faith and didn't hold back anything for themselves. We will never know how God engineered the situation behind the scenes to cause an unusual inheritance to land in this person's way. We do know that when we pray in desperation, it's a cry of faith and trust which God doesn't ignore. When we believe God for the impossible, He hears and He will act.

Faith where perseverance and persistence is necessary

When praying for individual situations, we have been amazed to see how God has responded. Sometimes persistence in faith is what God requires. I once prayed with a lady who was deaf in one ear. It's so easy to pray a simple prayer like this; "Oh Lord, please heal Joan's ear." It takes energy and the application of faith to persist in pressing through for answers which aren't always immediate.

Sometimes the Lord is looking for persistence and for us to engage our mind, will and emotions in intercession. He looks for how much we are prepared to do our part. This might mean us crying out to Him on behalf of another or commanding the enemy to leave the person or calling on the name of the Lord with all our heart.

On this particular occasion with the deaf lady, I was doing all three. I felt a righteous indignation that she should suffer in this way. She had already suffered enough from an extremely abusive background. I persisted in praying for around an hour. During this time, she didn't speak and neither I nor the team member with me felt we could leave her.

During this time of persisting and perseverance there came a moment when faith rose up in me. I sensed God was about to bring a breakthrough and my prayers, which included praying in tongues, became energized and fluent. I was praying things I had no mind to pray for. The ideas and thoughts flowed!

I knew the Holy Spirit was working in this situation and the full assurance came when the lady suddenly clasped her hand over her ear and bent double. I thought she was in pain but she managed to say, "Ouch, my ear is burning hot!" I knew God was at work and with this my faith rose further. "Thank You Lord for healing Joan, You are doing it and we agree with all You are doing. We love and bless You Lord for the healing You are bringing today. You are the Creator, the best doctor of the soul, the best surgeon. We trust You and Your faithfulness and power to set free and heal."

The words flowed on. Eventually, the lady sat up. She wanted to go out for a walk. Her countenance looked different and we knew God had done a work. I didn't need any evidence to tell me she had received healing because my spirit was bright and lifted. I felt none of the heaviness with which I had begun this healing session.

Faith had risen up in me and 'I knew that I knew' God had been at work. The lady came back beaming from ear to ear and told us that she had been unable to keep her hood up even though it was raining outside. The rain dropping on her hood was too noisy for her new-found hearing!

That breakthrough eventually came through persistent prayer. Sometimes it takes a while for our spirit to become energized with the power of God and for breakthroughs in faith to come. There are other times when God responds in spite of us and He takes us by surprise. It's just as well that none of us can place God in a box and make a technique or methodology out of Him!

Hindrances or blockages to faith

I spoke earlier of how, in this area of applying faith, we need to understand ourselves as much as we need to understand God. It's so easy to think that somehow we haven't met God's criteria for answered prayer.

Outlined below are some of the common hindrances or blockages to faith which we may struggle with.

a) Depression

Many people who come to our centers for help are suffering to one degree or another with depression. In this book I don't intend to go into all the details about depression and its roots. However, I do want to say that when someone comes for prayer about an area of their lives which is causing oppression and depression, it will be extremely hard for them to exercise faith.

A person who is depressed is low in their emotions and often crushed in spirit. There will be a variety of reasons why this is so and healing will be needed. However, in my experience, before the healing needs are addressed, the person needs our help to rise up in faith and in belief that God will change things for them. We must bring the person into the 'vertical' position of faith (even if they aren't able to express it at the time) rather than the 'horizontal' position which looks directly at the problem first.

I have found that by speaking out trust and belief in what God will do in front of the person and by bringing them into the presence of the Lord through praise, worship and trust of Him, the person's spirit begins to lift. God begins His work. When we verbalize our prayer with faith such as, "Lord, we know You are going to touch John today, You will bring Your restoration and healing and You are going to help him," it releases faith in him too.

When we articulate the mountain and speak about the freedom we believe Jesus has won and will bring, things begin to change in the spirit realm. When we speak this out confidently to the Lord and so that the powers of darkness can hear, it's as though a fight begins to take place. We could get disheartened by this fight but in fact it's good news because we know we are onto something important.

Pushing through in declared victory of all that Jesus has won for us is essential for breakthrough in prayer and bringing heaven down to earth. It may begin with words but as we press through, we will see God is doing things beyond what we could imagine.

For those in depression, it's very important that in an intercessory way, we are bringing them into the presence of the Lord. They are unable to get there themselves and need *our* prayer and engagement with the enemy to help them. The enemy holds depressed people bound because they are under a cloud of oppression and negativity which holds them back from engaging in prayer themselves. Their spirit which is crushed within them needs help to rise up.

Faith is something which 'catches on'. It's contagious. When it's exercised it grows stronger, and the stronger it becomes the more effective and powerful it is against the enemy and for seeing the Holy Spirit move in power.

b) Wrong Beliefs

As I said earlier, there are many hidden and subconscious beliefs we can hold which will hinder our trust and true faith in God.

We may for example, believe that God is uninterested in us and distant from us. This may come from having suffered neglect in childhood. We may not have received encouragement and affirmation in childhood which would give us the right confidence to approach God.

Our rightful needs may not have been met and neglect has left us suffering from lack of self worth and we therefore approach God from a position of begging Him to answer prayer rather than believing and trusting He has heard our prayer and is answering.

Others struggle with doubt and unbelief. This could be due to participation or training in other religions or the occult. Additionally, it could be because of intellectualism. We may be endeavoring to work it out with our minds and intellects. Rationalism stands in the way of faith as does skepticism and cynicism.

c) Sinful attitudes

We can hold attitudes which oppose faith. Our carnal or sinful nature will lead us to harbor un-forgiveness and bitterness. As a result there may be deep seated anger which gives way to resentment. When this is present, it will be impossible to reach out in faith and trust. There will be a barrier between us and God until this is repented of.

Self pity is an attitude which springs up when we see life's struggles through these spectacles. Everything will appear unfair, unjust, against us and with no positive view of the future.

Negativity goes along with self pity. Negative thinking and speaking comes out of our carnal (sinful) nature and envelops us if we give it room to thrive. We should be careful how we view others, how we speak about them or about our situation whether it's at home, family, work or ministry. The enemy is waiting to snatch words we use and pronouncements we make, to make them into realities.

Ingratitude is another area which gives no room for the Lord to work faith in our lives. It is an attitude whereby we see everything through pessimism and what we haven't had that we need. Gratitude to God and others releases faith and hope. When I was a child we used to sing a song that said, *'Count your blessings, count them one by one and it will surprise you what the Lord has done.'*

It's so true that when we express positive statements and attitudes, they release faith and they will come back to us in healthy ways. No-one wants to be in the company of people who moan and are full of negative thinking and behaving. Every one of us can find something to be grateful to the Lord for and for the ways that we are far better placed than many others.

Having a martyr type syndrome is associated with self pity and ingratitude. It projects onto others and God how badly done-by we believe we are. We have the attitude of believing we have tried so hard, we have done so much and no-one notices or bothers about us. It keeps us appeasing others in order to gain a sense of worth. It's difficult to apply any faith from this position.

Selfishness and greed are common attitudes which oppose the faith position. Rather than seeing the needs of others, we can become introverted and self focused or even self obsessed. It's good to have a healthy view and worth of self without which we can't love others. Romans 13:9 says, *'love your neighbor as yourself'*. However, if we are only concerned with our own needs and our own problems, we will give ground to the enemy to bind us in the area of faith. In fact the enemy is capable of sending things which will fulfill our self desires but aren't what we need and aren't the provision of God.

Harboring negative attitudes will keep us from walking in faith and trust. I remember praying with one person who, as soon as you combated one negative attitude, they would bring up another and then another. In the end you couldn't win, except to agree with them that there was no way out for them then!

All of these things need recognizing, confessing and repenting of. God wants to cleanse our hearts from the grave clothes which entangle us and keep us bound by sin. He wants us to call out to Him for His empowerment to change and He will do this for us if we are sincere.

d) Unhealed Areas

It could be that we struggle to gain victory in the areas above because we need to look at areas of our lives which still need healing and restoration. We have already outlined some of these.

If we have suffered deep abuses and injustices, we will have great difficulty truly trusting God and as a result faith will not come easily. The idea that God is loving and secure and faithful will seem like a fairytale which isn't true, even though with all our hearts we may want it to be true.

Trust in ourselves and others may have been shattered in childhood. At a deeper level, trust may never have been there as a foundation for us to grow from. Many have suffered such deep rejection in their earliest and formative years of life that trust isn't something which they have a framework for. Rather it is fear which has dominated their lifestyle and choices.

Rather than having freedom to live and breathe and move, mistrust has ensured that life is controlled by survival and living off your wits. With this kind of background, it's no wonder that there would be a massive struggle to believe and have faith in God for anything. Alternatively, there may be an unreality about faith whereby fantasy and illusions about God and what He will do are believed. It's easy when we have suffered deprivation to believe in a God of our own making in order to replace what has been lost.

Thankfully, God knows and sees our pain and He doesn't condemn, but He has provided a way for us to receive His healing and transformation, so we can identify the areas which need His freedom and begin to respond, grow and change. For anyone who wants to know more about help for unhealed areas, Ellel Ministries hold many healing retreats and courses designed to help.

Faith as a mustard seed

Thankfully God is not looking for superheroes. God looks for those who are teachable and who will reach out with faith which is even as small as a mustard seed. God says that even this amount of faith will say to the mountain "be removed" and it will!" (Luke 17:6).

In the whole area of applying faith as part of intercession, we can be encouraged that even the smallest amount of faith and trust in our covenantal, loving God will remove obstacles and move mountains. Let us come to Him in that place of humility with childlike trust and see how He will work out His purposes, remembering that we may well be part of the answer!

Soul Power

God created us in His image (Genesis 1:27). He is three in one –
Father, Son and Holy Spirit. We are created also in three parts: body,
soul and spirit. We see this, for example when Paul in Thessalonians
was praying for the believers and he prayed that they would be
whole in body, in soul and in spirit (1 Thessalonians 5:23).

Our body is the physical part of our being. It's through our body
that we appreciate our senses of sight, touch, sound, smell and
taste and it's through our bodies that we identify each other and
have the enjoyment of physical life here on earth. However, our
bodies are subject to this world's order and as such are subject to
decay and eventual death. Our bodies will return to dust one day.

On the other hand, as Christians our inner beings are being
renewed each day (2 Corinthians 4:16). God has placed eternity
in the heart of man (Ecclesiastes 3:11). We are primarily spiritual
beings and we will live on when our bodies decay and die!

This is the good news of the gospel – that through Jesus' death
and resurrection, we will live on with Him in eternity. One day,
we will all go to our home in glory! Jesus said, *"In my Father's house
there are many mansions, if it were not so I would have told you. I go to
prepare a place for you that where I am, you may be also."* (John 14:2).

While we are here on earth, it would be easy to forget that we
are primarily spiritual beings and we may be unaware that the
spiritual realms are real and that they affect us. We go about our

normal lives which are made up of physical activity, without realizing that there are spiritual laws as well as physical laws.

What is the soul? Our souls are designed by God to mirror the workings of our spirit. Our spirits contain our life-giving energy source which receives the new birth. In turn our spirits express that life through our soul. Our soul is the part of us which contains our mind, our will and our emotions and it expresses the life of the spirit. The Greek word for soul is *psyche*.

Our mind contains what we think. Our will is where we decide to do something about what we think and our emotions are the feelings which come alongside as a result of what we think and the choices we make. For example, my body may be in need of food. With my will I decide to cook something and with my emotions I feel happy at the thought of something I like being made for me to eat.

In Romans 7:14-23, Paul speaks about a battle between our soul and our spirit. In our spirit we may want to do the right thing and to obey God and follow His ways but this may be opposed by a part of our sin nature in the soul area which wants and demands the opposite!

The reality is that we all have this battle to some degree or another. Because of our sinful nature, we struggle to live as a spiritual man in perfect relationship with Creator God. If we still lived in the Garden of Eden, we wouldn't have such problems. However, we live in a fallen world where sin and decay have entered and we have an enemy who is the god of this world who contends for anything conceived by God.

We ourselves are fallen and fallible and as such we are subject to temptation. It would be easy not to sin if sin wasn't something we wanted! However, from the moment we are conceived we all want our own way and our responses reflect this. We know that we are incapable of perfect responses, reactions and choices.

Adam and Eve in the Garden of Eden were living in perfect harmony with God and yet with their free-will choice they still made the decision to take matters into their own hands. In their souls, they thought they knew better. They saw the forbidden tree with its fruit and thought (using their soul power) "why shouldn't we taste of this fruit?" They mistrusted God and the sin of pride entered their hearts. They rose up and tried to be above God.

Their souls won the battle, they took what they wanted and enjoyed it, but to the expense of their higher good and need. In obeying their souls they forfeited their relationship with God. This should be enough to warn each of us of the danger of soul power.

Soul power is in effect using our natural or carnal thinking to make sense of the divine. It's where we haven't come into submission to Him wanting His way, His mind and His will. For Adam and Eve it meant dire consequences because they lost their relationship with God at that point. They had walked away from their place of safety and protection which was the place of submission to God.

This is our position as fallen mankind. Thank God that He saw man's plight and He intervened, sending a part of Himself, His Son Jesus, to open up the way for restoration of our relationship with Him and for us to receive all that He intended for us. Nevertheless, we haven't returned to the time of the Garden of Eden (the earth before death and decay entered) and we still live with the effects of the fall and as such we always have to win the battle that Paul speaks of in Romans between our soul and our spirit.

'Soulish' praying

Early on in the journey of learning how God heals and restores people's lives, we came across this area of soul power and 'soulish' prayers. We were involved in setting an individual free from high occult power. Battles raged incessantly as there were many strongholds and legal rights the enemy had gained during this person's lifetime and in her generation line.

I was on a steep learning curve. My own background had not prepared me to understand the horrific abuses and traumas which surrounded this situation. Looking back I am so grateful to God that He filled me with His compassion and gave me the ability and capacity to keep going against all odds. However, there were countless times when I wanted to give up. It was so hard.

We had many people praying for us as a team. The battles raged through day and night and in the stark reality of normal life it made no sense at all. Yet we continued to see victories won and we were learning many principles and keys which in retrospect, we now see have been used to set thousands free.

God had His wisdom in taking us through this time of testing and learning. In our natural minds, it was crazy. To many looking on, it appeared wrong. The natural mind came into play. It wasn't right to work all those hours. Many others could have benefited more in the time we spent with just one person. Families were being neglected. The work was being neglected. It wasn't right for the team to get so exhausted. These thoughts and many others were occupying our minds too!

There came a time when it was increasingly difficult to see breakthrough and freedom come in the individual's life. We simply couldn't understand why the battle was so hard and why we would go through hours of nothing happening when we prayed. We cried out to God for keys and answers but were met with silence.

During one of the breaks, I had gone away from the situation and spent some time chatting with a few folk who were around Ellel Grange at the time. One lady spoke with me and said very sincerely, "we have set up an intercession team and we are asking God to stop this ministry and to release you all and give you a rest and a holiday." I was quite taken aback. This lady didn't have a wrong heart and she was full of sympathy for us but something in my spirit felt uneasy.

As I went back into the ministry session, I felt the Lord challenge me personally on whether this was what I wanted. Of course my body and soul most definitely wanted to have a rest and a break and yet I also knew that unless it was God bringing this about, I didn't want to be disobedient. I found myself saying to the Lord, "if it's Your perfect will that we continue for now, I will trust You to bring about the time for rest and I will trust You for strength to continue."

It was then that I realized that one of the reasons the ministry had become so prolonged was because of the intercession going on which was not in accordance with God's will. I became aware that Satan hears those 'soulish' intercessions and he adds his power of agreement to them. Of course, he wanted nothing better than for us to give up and to go home for a rest.

This was his plan to get us out of doing this ministry. However, we were being worn out fighting against a power in prayer which was intended to help but in reality was doing the opposite. Satan's plan was dangerous because if the person had gone home prematurely and not received the deliverance and freedom they needed at that time, they would have been extremely vulnerable to spiritual and physical attacks.

Finally, as I shared these insights with the team who were ministering, we prayed and asked the Lord to cut us free from 'soulish' praying and intercession. We forgave those who had mistakenly taken matters into their own hands. They had not understood the power of the soul. We then sensed the Lord send His angels to warfare on our behalf. As a result the anointing of God returned, we ourselves were filled with energy and a vital battle was won. We were able to take our rest based on God's timing and with great freedom and rejoicing.

This was a very important lesson in how our ('soulish') human affection and compassion can stand in the way of God's purposes. When we turn these into prayers we need to be very careful that we aren't praying in opposition to God and unwittingly strengthening the hand of the enemy. We need to remember we have an enemy who is waiting to take our 'soulish' agreements, even if they are spoken in prayer form and use them for his ends. He looks for our agreement with him which gives him power to bind things here on earth.

The right prayer for the team in these circumstances would have been to pray that the Lord would strengthen us, give us grace and also give us wisdom and keys for the breakthrough needed. We needed warfare prayers that the tactics of the enemy would be exposed. Although I hated this lesson and it was very hard at the time, I am now extremely grateful to God for teaching us about this area because it revealed a powerful key in releasing the power of God here on earth.

God wants to use our human understanding and he gave us our minds and intellects to use. He doesn't, however, want us to put all our faith and trust in human logic. He desires that we look to Him for His wisdom, His mind and His way. What makes sense to us may not be the way God wants to work.

To walk with Him and partner with Him in the supernatural journey of faith, we will need to learn submission to His higher ways. Although God will use our human logic and our minds, we shouldn't be dependent on them but depend on *Him* who works in ways that defy human reasoning.

We also need to learn that God uses the weak and foolish things of this world to confound the wise! He turns the ways of man upside down. We only need to look at the way the Son of God entered the world. Everyone was looking for Him to arrive at a palace in a place of kingship. It never entered the heart of man that God would come in the form of a baby to a lowly mother and where there was no room for Him to be born. This was God's perfect wisdom!

In our walk with God we will learn that He turns the way of the world upside down. He is the infallible and we are fallible. He is infinite and we are finite. The sooner we come to Him in humility to learn His ways, the sooner we will have the joy and freedom of watching Him at work and sharing in it.

God's ways are foolishness to the world. For instance 'the way up is the way down', 'the key to receiving is giving away', *'when we are weak then we are strong'*, *'when we are foolish then we are wise'* and *'for us to die is to gain life!'*

Unless the spirit of God empowers and enables our spiritual life, it would be easy to live in the natural realms and perhaps never see what God really is able to do through us. We could even hinder the work of God.

We need understanding that our passivity, our human and natural way of thinking and choosing, can release soul power which does not remain 'dormant' but can be set alight by the enemy and used for negative purposes. It can become the enemy of God's purposes. The 'soulish' answer may be a popular one and in fact most of the time it is.

God doesn't make it easy to find Him. His way is the best way but it's rather like treasure. It doesn't come easily. God tests us to see whether we truly want His way or whether we would prefer the easy way. The way which our souls like is the way where there's no price, discomfort or struggle. The highest way is the way of holiness where God wants to release His glory within us.

However the way of testing is a way of proving us, whether our faith is genuine and real. Sometimes we come to God in a 'soulish' way. We come to Him for what we can get, what we need and what suits us. We can't treat God like this and we will never manipulate God. He simply allows us to go our way. It causes Him pain but He has to allow us to use our free will and if we want things our way, He will let us go our way.

Testing is God's way of refining us and bringing out the gold within us. His desire is that we be free from the grave clothes of 'soulish' living and find that as we come into rightful submission to Him, we discover the abundant life Jesus won for us (John 10:10).

In essence, God desires that we come to an end of our way of fixing life and of making things work for ourselves and others and that we step into His way. This requires that, in relationship with Him, our spirits be released to bow the knee to His way. Without His way, we will find ourselves without the keys which will bring about transformation.

Soul power in relationships

The team were once ministering to someone who had been receiving very good medical care but the medics came to an end of what they could do. The lady came to Ellel Grange for help and attended one of our Healing Retreats. At the end of the retreat she was so much better that her husband, church members and the medical staff recognized something wonderful had taken place.

The lady came many times for further periods of healing and each time God brought more healing and restoration. However, because this went on for longer than people in her church thought it should, there began to be questions asked as to whether she should be attending ministry sessions anymore.

One day when we were praying with this particular lady, we felt we were hitting a brick wall. The lady herself kept saying she felt she shouldn't be there, she was wasting our time, we should disbelieve her and tell her to leave! None of this made sense to us. However, she persisted and finally told us that she thought we didn't know what we were doing and she should go back home.

After a while we came to realize that this sudden turnaround in her attitude was coming from her soul. It was as though there was no connection to her spirit. She was unable to pray and no spark of faith came from her. She was caught up in a completely human perspective of her condition.

We tried to battle against the enemy in an attempt to see change. This was to no avail. Eventually, the Lord reminded us that she could be suffering under the weight of soul power in the spirit realm. We began to pray differently and asked the Lord to send his angels to surround the room and to take away from her spirit any human judgments or 'soulish' agreements or prayers that were being directed towards her and used by the enemy to draw her away from what the Lord had for her.

As soon as we prayed this prayer, the lady became aware of powerful words that were telling her what to do. It was clear that they were coming from beliefs and judgments and powers of agreement which the powers of darkness were using effectively to slow down and even stop the flow of anointing in the ministry situation.

When we are praying, we need to be careful that we are directing our prayers to where God is seated in the heavenly realms high over all. This is the 'vertical' prayer position. If our eyes are on the 'horizontal' position of the natural realm and we are looking for God in this place, we could easily waste much time and effort. We could be praying from the soul rather than from the Spirit of God energizing, touching and empowering our spirit. The enemy loves this kind of praying. It doesn't threaten him at all.

We have learnt to pray this prayer of asking the Lord to take away any soul power which is affecting situations where we need a breakthrough and particularly if we are struggling without one.

Christian soul power

The enemy is particularly after Christian soul power. If Christians come together and pray for something in Christ's name which isn't in line with His will and purpose and in fact has wrong intent within it, the enemy will use it to attack those against whom the prayer is targeted. If he can gain the agreement and co-operation of Christians then he has the highest source of power imaginable.

I remember a time when in our early and growing years as a ministry, there were some Christians who were in strong disagreement with us. They had many reasons to be wary and for some, their response was to remain distant. This was perhaps the right position to be in because they were rightfully testing the ministry and weren't ready to expose themselves or others to it.

However, others didn't remain distant but became antagonistic and verbal in their attacks against the ministry and those within it. One of the greatest miracles of Ellel Ministries today is that we withstood these attacks from the place of completely trusting the Lord, not with our own defenses. Our only armor was forgiveness and allowing God to defend us. If the work was truly His, He would vindicate.

It grieves the Lord when we take up a 'soulish' defense of ourselves or alternatively when we attempt to defend Him. This is soul power wrapped up as a 'righteous attack.' We are attempting to win a victory but are in fact doing this 'soulishly'. If we add weight to these attacks on others with our prayers and worse still, if we invite other people to join in our offense and our praying, this will give power and many rights to the enemy. And it will create pain, suffering and division in the body of Christ.

'Soulish' words

Words are very powerful. The bible tells us that words can bring life or they can bring death (Proverbs 18:21). We should be very careful when we speak or pray that we are not making agreements which the enemy can use. This is closely aligned to making judgments. When we make 'soulish' agreements and judgments, the enemy can use them against us and against others.

For instance we may speak out and say things such as, "that person will never amount to anything" or "that ministry will fail soon" or "God will never use so and so." These statements come from our soul rather than from the heart of God and His Spirit within us.

If we say these things to someone else and they agree with us, there is power in the agreement which the enemy detects and which gives him rights. The things we said can form a curse of words and be used against the person or ministry like the fiery darts the Scripture speaks of. They can unleash death (possibly physical but mainly spiritual and emotional), decline and sickness into a person or a group of people.

We have learnt to warfare over any assaults of soul power which might be being launched against us, either directly from the enemy or from a person or group of people. It is important to do that because these 'soulish' assaults unleash spiritual power which the enemy can use.

'Soulish' influence

We all have influence over someone else from time to time. We can use this influence in a godly way or in an ungodly and unwise way. If we only have partial or half truth, we can cause someone else to believe something very far from the truth. This is a breeding ground for the enemy. He is the father of lies and he feeds on manipulation of truth creating falsehood and then perpetrating it.

It is therefore important that we become aware of how we use our influence which can come out of our soul. This could show itself as intellectual arguments or emotional displays of hurt (anger or pain) which in turn cause another to take offense on our behalf and to defend us. It's not difficult to sway others in this area and to cause them to take up our beliefs thus creating a 'soulish' power of agreement.

Gifting

We have probably all come across a person who has great gifting and talent. They say that they want to use this gifting to serve God and their words seem very sincere. However, as time has gone on it comes to light that their gifting and personality do not match their character. In these situations, personality power comes into play, and the person uses their gifting to encourage others into joining them or believing them.

Our personalities are given to us by God but if we use them to persuade and influence people in order to meet our agenda or to dominate them in some way we are stepping over a line of what is safe. Power is something that God gives but if we use it wrongly then we unleash the power of the soul and ultimately can give Satan power. A person may begin with good intentions but if they use their personality to gain more credence, position, influence or power, then in extreme cases the power of the soul can even become a demonic force.

Having 'People Power' is a word for something that is quite common- using the soul to influence people. The person has a need for significance and worth which is sought in the wrong places and as a result they look for methods which bring popularity. Some may find they have a talent to make people laugh, others may have a persuasive way of speaking, they may be a born leader, or they may be the life and soul of the party and many more.

None of these things are wrong in themselves but when they are used 'soulishly' in order to sway people, the boundary lines are crossed into an ungodly use of the soul which is dangerous. It can end up with the enemy being at work, bringing about persuasion and eventually control, deception and division.

Sexuality

The gift of sexuality is a perfect 'breeding ground' for Satan to appeal to the soul. The temptation is to use our looks, our personality or our body to gain power, gain acceptance, receive comfort or to manipulate another. This is an area where a massive amount of healing is needed.

Unfortunately we are constantly helping people who are in bondage due to ungodly sexual experiences. Setting them free will involve prayer for them to be cut free from the soul power controlling them, which in turn has brought about spiritual bondage.

Soul power from groups

When a group of people come together collectively in agreement over anything, this can be extremely powerful. In the physical realms these are called committees or councils! The same power is reflected in the spiritual realms and there will be a battle for authority.

When collective godly decisions are made, this will result in blessings coming down to earth affecting many lives for good. Alternatively, when collective decisions are ungodly and out of line with created order and God's truth, cursing will come down and affect many as a result.

What we begin to see here is the makings of a territorial power. During a prayer ministry time for a lady who had been sexually abused, we became aware of her personality changing. This was more than a mood swing. When we spoke with her she said that she felt she was being held by spiritual cords which were making her feel she wanted the abuse and belonged somewhere different than with us.

We began to see that the powers of darkness were receiving their power from the authority and power of a human group. It seemed this group was pulling her back using soul power connected to the place of their operation. We had no authority to deal with the overall territorial power but we did have authority to ask Jesus to set the lady free from the group who were empowering this and to cut the spiritual cords holding her. When we did so she immediately felt as though her own personality had returned. She had been experiencing an overlay of other people's personality power.

Here is an example of a prayer to be set free from soul power which may be affecting you personally or your family, friends, business, church, or ministry.

"Thank You Jesus for shedding Your blood, dying and rising again, that I might be set free. I ask You to forgive me for my sins and to cleanse me from all unrighteousness.

I now freely forgive all those who have made 'soulish' judgments, agreements or prayers about me or my . . . .(insert family, business, or church). I ask You to bless them and release them from my life and my. . . . (family etc).

I repent of coming under and submitting to the influence of individuals or groups who have controlled my thoughts and therefore my attitudes, beliefs and decisions in ungodly ways. I now release these people into the freedom of my forgiveness.

Please release Your heavenly host to do battle on my behalf and to take away from me (and my. . . .) all effects of people or groups who are using soul power knowingly or unknowingly, with or without malice to control and dominate my life. Please cut every ungodly tie to them and their words and actions. In Jesus' name I take up my authority to rebuke and cast out any demonic power that has placed me (or my. . . .) in bondage as a result."

We have found it very powerful to redress the words which will have been specifically used against us with the truth. For example, "I ask you Lord to take away the soul power affecting me that comes from every person who has said or done things against me and who may be speaking out against me (or my. . . .) or agreeing with others about me (or my. . . .) in an ungodly way."

Mention specifically the kind of words which may have been used such as, "they will be bankrupt soon", "they will never survive this", "she/he will die", "he/she belongs in a mental institution", "they are not sane", "pray them out" etc. In prayer, it is important to redress the words of curse with the opposite e.g. *"I will not die but live and declare the wondrous deeds of the Lord'*. We speak life into... (name) and thank you Lord that you have a destiny purpose to be fulfilled."

Finally, we should remember that Jesus said, *"bless those who curse you and pray for those who despitefully use you"* (Luke 6:28). This is the antidote to soul power coming against us. It is hard to bless those who hurt us and to imagine them being blessed. However, it's part of our walk in forgiveness. Jesus also said, *"judge not, that you yourself be not judged"* (Matthew 7:1) and *"love and forgive your enemies"* (Matthew 6:14).

Jesus will give us the enabling and grace to forgive and it is from this place that we can ask Him to bless those who curse us. This does *not* mean that God will let those who have hurt us go free. They remain under His judgment. We have trusted Jesus who is the only righteous and fair judge. It's from this place that we are truly set free from their influence and from the power of the enemy.

We can effectively help others who suffer from being in this position. We will be undoing the work of the enemy and will be living in the victory Jesus has won for us.

Called to Battle and War

We can't avoid looking at the work of Satan and his power as our enemy if we are going to be an effective part of bringing God's kingdom here on earth as it is in heaven.

Jesus, in Luke's gospel, left us in no doubt about the commission He was giving us as His disciples, to *'proclaim the gospel, heal the sick and cast out demons'* (Luke 9:1-2).

When we belong to Jesus, we have in effect begun a war! We have made a clear declaration as to which side we are on. We can't afford to be complacent. Of course, the enemy is quite happy if we sit back and remain unchanged by our Christian faith. We don't present any problem to him. However, if we are active and we participate in furthering the kingdom of God, although we can expect battles and contention, we will see victories won.

If we are disciples of the Lord Jesus Christ who desire to see His kingdom come on earth as it is in heaven, we can't ignore the fact that we are called to be part of the answer. The bible teaches us that God hates it when we are complacent and comfortable and we are neither cold nor hot (Revelation 3:15).

It's when we truly begin to change and move out of our comfort zone into doing the works of the kingdom that Satan takes note. We are engaging in a battle and therefore it's vital that we understand what we have agreed to. If we remain in ignorance, complacency and passivity, we won't bear fruit. John 15:16 says, *'You did not choose me but I chose you, and I appointed you to go and bear fruit, fruit that will last, so that the Father will give you whatever you ask in My name'.*

We are destined by the Lord to bring home to him baskets of fruit which has been borne out of our lives being yielded to Him and to His purposes. The enemy contends our fruitfulness. He hates it because it's this which causes the kingdom of God to grow and it's this fruit which strips him of his power. In our place of intercession (bringing forth God's purposes here on earth) we will experience contention. Everything that's conceived by the heart of God is contended for. Therefore we need to know the nature of the battle and be prepared.

God knows that Satan will endeavor to use us and to sift us. Luke 22:31 tells us that Jesus said, *'Simon, Simon, listen! Satan has demanded to sift all of you like wheat but I have prayed for you that your own faith may not fail'.*

We can be encouraged that although God will allow Satan to challenge and test us, Jesus Himself is praying for us. He is our Intercessor coming before the Father on our behalf. Even when we go through the fire and trials of our faith, we will not be tempted or tested beyond that which we can endure (1 Corinthians 10:13).

Jesus has won the victory over the powers of darkness and we are seated with Him. We have been given power and authority in Jesus' name over the enemy.

It's in the name of Jesus that we can begin to plunder the kingdom of darkness and usher in the kingdom of God with light and truth. However, in doing so, we should be aware that just as there is a protocol in God's kingdom, there is also a protocol in Satan's kingdom. Don't be deceived into thinking that the powers of darkness are disorganized and chaotic. They are not, although the truth is that the *fruit* of Satan's kingdom is confusion, chaos and destruction.

It's important that, understanding how Satan and the powers of darkness operate, we don't overstep our lines of authority and the boundaries God has set.

a) We can't treat Satan and demons in a cavalier and disrespect-
    ful way. We should remember that the enemy has rights
    and power. He is the god of this world (2 Corinthians 4:4)
    and the whole earth is currently under his rule (1 John 5:19).
    Some people treat Satan as someone who can be mocked
    and laughed at. We shouldn't put the enemy to the test or
    play games of any kind with him.

b) The enemy has power and we can't treat him as though he
    has no ability to bother us or harm us. Our place of safety is
    in Christ. Jesus Himself knew the power of the enemy and
    didn't dialogue with him, other than to put Satan firmly
    where he belonged and under authority.

c) We can tell the enemy to leave our lives or another person's
    life (only with their agreement) if we have made sure all the
    rights the enemy have been dealt with. We should remem-
    ber that if we try and command the enemy to leave when
    there is still un-confessed sin, deeply unhealed areas or con-
    trolling fear present, he may not leave.

d) There is a protocol in the supernatural realms. Satan sees
    if we are not under proper spiritual authority and if we are
    isolated. We could be vulnerable and open ourselves up to
    attack.

When we look at the prayer of battle, we are talking about engaging with the enemy. We don't *pray* to the enemy but in prayer we
can *speak* to the enemy and give him orders in the name of Jesus.
We can also speak and declare truth to the enemy.

Remember, we are seated with Jesus in the heavenly places and
have been given authority over the enemy. First, we have to recognize where he is at work. Sometimes this will be obvious but
at other times it will be more subtle as he tries to use our flesh to
draw us into spiritual agreements with him.

'*We do not wage war against flesh and blood but against the powers
and principalities of this dark age*' (Ephesians 6:12). The bible tells
us '*not to be ignorant of Satan's devices*'. One of the devices Satan
uses is to keep us ignorant. If we remain ignorant then he can

carry out his plans and objectives unchallenged, unexposed and un-dealt with.

Passivity

Another device Satan uses is for us to be complacent and passive. From this position, we see difficulties, struggles and impossibilities - but do nothing. It could be that we pray and ask God to intervene. However, we forget that God has given us the authority and power in His name to rise up in battle against the enemy and win the victory in the name of Jesus.

When praying for the people who come to our centers in bondage, we often have to teach them the prayer of battle! It's so easy from the position of rational thinking (the soul area) to find that we rationalize a spiritual problem or even that we try to 'inner heal' demonic power.

This book is not about deliverance ministry. My husband Peter has written a book on that subject for those who need or want to know about this area of ministry. It's called *Healing through Deliverance*. However, it's an important part of intercession to know how to rise up against the powers of darkness affecting the situations we are praying for.

It's easy to put the blame onto people for something the enemy has initiated and perpetrated. The other side of the coin can also be true and there are some people who blame demons for everything and don't look at their own responsibility. I am talking here about redressing the balance where there is ignorance of Satan's ways or there is complacency. Sometimes it can even be unbelief!

Jesus was quick to identify the tactics of His enemy and he rose up against Satan. We need to do the same. If we see the imprint of the enemy in our life or in the lives of our family, church or community, the work of the Holy Spirit within us will bring a sense of righteous indignation and anger. This is what the Lord uses to stir us up out of complacency to prayer and battle!

There will be a power behind what is happening and we should take up our authority and rise up with a righteous indignation and speak to the enemy. "Enemy, I recognize you, I see what you are doing, I take authority over you in the name of Jesus and I tell you to *stop* now."

For example we may say on behalf of another: "In Jesus' name we rebuke you and your works in John's life", "John is not going to give up, John is being changed and strengthened by Jesus, we are standing with John, you will not continue your torment."

In effect we are speaking directly to the powers of darkness. We are declaring God's truth for ourselves or for the person we are ministering to. We are not saying these words passively. We are rising up with an authority in our voice and making powerful declarations and agreements.

I was once praying with a lady who was very depressed and suicidal. It seemed that she had nothing to withstand the attacks of the enemy and she was relentlessly tormented with thoughts of what she saw as her failure and worthlessness. As much as we tried to help this lady rise up in her own spirit and speak out truth to the enemy, she was unable to do so.

Once some healing and deliverance had taken place in her life and we had prayed on her behalf and spoken the prayer of battle to the enemy, she began to become stronger in her spirit. We taught her how to rise up and speak things out directly herself to the enemy.

At first she was most reluctant and hesitant and we began to think it was due to her being self-conscious. However, we soon discerned that this in itself was a tactic of the enemy who was doing all he could to hold her back from speaking out words of truth and light. If she did so and we placed our agreement to it, the enemy would lose his grip and a victory would be won in Jesus' name.

We soon learned that the prayer of battle is one of the most important prayers in our armory. When we speak out loud the truths Jesus has given us, they are open declarations into the heavenly realms. When others agree with us, then they are powerful for the bringing down of strongholds. It is worth noting that the word 'amen' is a powerful word because it actually means, 'so let it be'. When we speak out 'amen' to words of truth and light, the agreement is sealed in the spirit realm.

There are many hymns and songs today which contain words and prayers of battle. These are effective in ushering in the anointing of the Lord. Some examples are *'All hail the lamb... His praise shall be our battle cry'*), *'In Heavenly armor we enter the land, the battle belongs to the Lord'*, *'Onward Christian Soldiers, marching on to war with the cross of Jesus going on before'*, *'The Lord has given a land of good things... we'll march right on to the victory side.'*

We are bringing heaven down to earth and as we sing and speak out truth the powers of darkness are made to hear. They know they are losing ground as we do this. They hate the truth of Scripture being held against them.

When we are engaged in battle against the enemy, it is of course vital we remember our armor (Ephesians chapter 6). There are many books written with explanations on this passage in Ephesians. Here, I am giving a simple explanation which I have found helpful myself and as I teach people to understand and apply these principles.

Firstly, we are not just saying some words each day as though the words themselves are magic. People have said to me, "I prayed today and put on my armor and I am still being attacked." Wearing our armor is living out the reality of who we are in Christ Jesus. The enemy sees this and knows when we are speaking words alone and not living the truth of those words.

> *Be strong in the Lord and in the strength of his power. Put on the whole armor of God, so that you may be able to stand against the wiles of the devil. For our struggle is not against enemies of blood and flesh, but against the rulers, against the powers of this present darkness, against the spiritual forces of evil in the heavenly places.*
>
> *Therefore take up the whole armor of God, so that you may be able to withstand on that evil day, and having done everything, to stand firm.*
>
> Ephesians 6:10-13

The Helmet of Salvation

Many are wearing the opposite of armor, often because of unhealed areas in their lives. The helmet of doubt is one such opposite. When we ask a person if they are assured of their salvation, they may answer, "I hope so" or "I think so." God wants us to be secure in our relationship with him and to deal with any issues which cast doubt on this. This is closing the door to the enemy.

The Breastplate of Righteousness

The breastplate of righteousness is of course our righteousness in Christ Jesus, but it can't be worn if we are walking with deliberate and known unrighteous living which needs cleansing. We may think of sin as being the big areas such as adultery, murder, and stealing but often subtle sins are the more common ones. They make us vulnerable to attack.

The subtle areas of unrighteousness are our pride, our lack of submission, our malicious tongue, our deceit, bitterness and selfishness. The Lord looks on our heart and if we desire to be cleansed and holy before him, He covers us but if we don't, then we will give the enemy grounds to attack us, especially any weak areas within us.

When we have unhealed areas in our lives, our carnal nature is easily stirred up for sinful purposes. Our hurts and pains give life to our carnality and it's easy to respond in fleshly ways. That's why healing is important. Healing brings victory over our sinful or carnal nature as we are freed to respond out of love and trust in God rather than out of fear, unbelief and self protection.

The Belt of Truth

The truth we are being told to wear is the truth of God's word.

Indeed, the word of God is living and active, sharper than any two-edged sword, piercing until it divides soul from spirit, joints from marrow; it is able to judge the thoughts and intentions of the heart.
(Hebrews 4:12)

The opposite of truth is falsehood, deceit and lies. We have discovered in the healing ministry that it's common to find people who deep down inside believe fundamental falsehood and lies about themselves. Such lies may include: "I'm a failure", "God doesn't love me", "I'm a mistake", "I'm bad", "Nobody wants me", and "I'm dirty".

Outwardly, we say we agree with Scripture and we do, but there is often an inward belief which doesn't line up. I describe this as a 'core' belief because it comes from our inner core. Because there is a conflict within us we then become *'double minded and unstable in all our ways'* as it says in the bible (James 1:8).

The enemy sees these unbiblical 'core' beliefs and he uses them to torment us with false guilt. This is the reason why so many people come to us asking how it is that although they are Christians, they come under such attack. The reason is that the enemy has rights because of unhealed areas of pain and hurt. They are living with deeply held beliefs which affect their relationship with others and with God Himself.

The Sword of the Spirit

The sword of the spirit is what it says, which is "sharp." We will be ineffective and open to enemy attack if we are not *living* in the reality of the Word of God, even if we are unable to quote chapter and verse from it. The enemy knows when we speak out truth from the Word of God and from our relationship with Jesus. He also knows when we mean it.

The Holy Spirit within us will prompt us to use this part of our armor to plunder the enemy and take ground from him. However, if our sword is blunt, we won't gain the ground and may even lose ground. We shall have to win back this ground.

The Shield of Faith

When we walk in unbelief and doubt, we can't please God.

Ask in faith, never doubting, for the one who doubts is like a wave of the sea, driven and tossed by the wind.

(James 1:6).

I shall speak more about the subject of faith in another chapter of this book, but it should be emphasized at this point that faith is a shield against the enemy.

Once again, he sees and knows our true position in Christ. Saying the words is not enough. God releases His power when we trust Him fully and with all our hearts.

For the doubter is double-minded and unstable in every way and must not expect to receive anything from the Lord.

(James 1:8).

Shoes Clad with the Gospel of Peace

Our shoes are what we walk in. They take the weight of our body and protect us from the ground.

And the peace of God, which surpasses all understanding, will guard your hearts and your minds in Christ Jesus.

(Philippians 4:7).

He Himself is our peace.

(Ephesians 2:14).

Jesus Himself said in John 14: 27, '*Peace I leave with you; my peace I give to you. I do not give to you as the world gives. Do not let your hearts be troubled, and do not let them be afraid*'.

The enemy will have the right to oppress, attack, contend and threaten us when we are not wearing our armor which is the peace of Christ in our hearts. The opposite of peace is fear. When we walk in fear, we are walking without shoes. We will live with hurts, struggles, problems and setbacks.

On a daily basis, we are ministering to people who are held in bondage to fear. Fear leads to control and control leads to protecting ourselves. When we protect ourselves, we move away from God's protection. The good news is that Jesus sets the captives free from fear.

Fear opposes trust in our heavenly Father and causes us to walk in insecurity. The Lord wants to heal areas of our lives that have been held in bondage and to liberate us so that we can truly live with deep peace and security in our hearts whatever our circumstances are.

We find it tremendously sad when we meet Christians who love God and are seeking to serve Him with all their lives, yet their hearts are troubled and even tormented. This is not how God intended us to live and He has given us the remedy in healing us and setting us free.

In conclusion, we have been given the keys, the armor and the tools to battle in the spirit realm against the powers of darkness. The battle belongs to the Lord and our place is to stand firm in the strength of His might and to participate in battling with Him to bring forth the victory Jesus has won for us.

The Gift of Discernment

In the New Testament we see that Jesus knew His enemy, recognized the works of the enemy and He also spoke to the enemy. On one such occasion, Jesus was telling His disciples that He must go to Jerusalem and undergo great suffering. Simon Peter remonstrated with Jesus and rebuked him saying in Matthew 16:22, *"God forbid it, Lord. This must never happen to you."* Jesus, in verse 23, recognized the voice of the enemy, turned towards Simon Peter and said directly to the enemy, *"get behind me Satan."*

Jesus knew that through Simon Peter's words of disagreement with the will of God and in his pain and indignation, the enemy was trying to manipulate Him into agreeing to something outside His Father's will. In fact, this is a very good example of soul power at work. Simon Peter was endeavoring to influence and help Jesus by fixing the situation with natural man's way. The enemy wanted to snatch the opportunity to trick Jesus into agreeing to an easier way!

In Matthew 16:23, Jesus went on to say to Simon Peter, *"You are a stumbling block to me; for you are setting your mind not on divine things but on human things."* This is a lesson to us that we can all be used to speak out and declare things from our soul which the enemy is behind and will use. In the previous chapter, we looked at soul power and the way our natural and human thinking can be used by the enemy to stand against God's purposes by influencing and affecting others, as well as ourselves. In this example, Jesus discerned that a demonic spirit was speaking through one of His disciples.

If the enemy attempted to use one of the disciples closest to Jesus and to a degree he succeeded, then we should be warned and be aware that the enemy will attempt to use any of us. Jesus used His perfect discernment to put the enemy under authority and to rebuke Simon Peter for speaking out words against the perfect will of His Father.

Discernment is a gift of the Holy Spirit. Many of the other gifts of the Holy Spirit are regularly taught and exercised such as prophecy, tongues, the gift of faith, tongues, and knowledge (1 Corinthians 12:4-11). However, we desperately need to know more about exercising the gift of discernment in the body of Christ today. Without recognizing the way the enemy works and discerning his plan and strategy, we will be like those who go to war without armory and weapons ('do not be ignorant of Satan's devices' 2 Corinthians 2:11).

Through our healing retreats, training courses and schools, we regularly teach and minister in the area of healing and discipleship. Healing and discipleship can't be separated if we are to be fully effective in God's purposes. We pray with Christians who are gripped by fear and insecurity, addictions, relationship issues, depression and many other areas which hold them back from the abundant life Jesus came to win for them (John 10:10).

We teach how to recognize the powers of darkness, how to battle and gain the victory. God wants to reveal to us the strategy of the enemy so that with Him and in the power of His Spirit, we can plunder Satan's kingdom and release those who are captive to it. We also need to discern what God is doing. The gift of discernment is critical for us to be effective in prayer and to move forward in His purposes.

Fallen discernment

Many years ago, we had a visiting minister who came from New Zealand to speak with our team. His name was Tom Marshall; he has now gone to be with the Lord. One of the things he spoke about remained with me and gave me a vital understanding of myself. Tom told us that criticism was in fact 'fallen discernment.' It was at this time that I understood that to critique something well was using discernment and that criticism in itself was not sinful. It was originally designed by God to be one of the most helpful and necessary gifts of all. I also became aware that criticism coming from the sinful nature will tear down and destroy and in fact will do the work of the enemy.

My nature tends towards the artistic and creative side rather than the scientific and logical. An artistic person has to be able to critique his or her work in order to become dissatisfied and then to begin to wrestle with it in order to change and grow. This is all part of growing in gifting but it can be pretty painful because we live in a fallen condition.

The enemy, as we know, wants to condemn us and he uses our God-given gift of being able to critique in order to do it. He points his accusatory finger at us and speaks words of condemnation into our hearts. He feeds any sense of our failure, our frustration, our self hatred and self loathing. If he could, he would have us believe and agree with him that we are complete rubbish, no good and worthless. The very gift God has given us as mankind, the enemy would seek to steal and use for his ends!

True ability to discern

God is our Creator. We are *'fearfully and wonderfully made'* (Psalm 139:14). The bible, in Genesis, says that God looked at what He had made (humankind) and said, *"it is good"* (Genesis 1:31). We are not rubbish in God's eyes. This is His judgment! It's imperative that we align ourselves with the truth revealed in His Word. It's from this place that our true ability to critique (discern) will come. From a healing and discipleship perspective this will take time as we grow, with our inner beliefs being transformed and changed into the truth of God's Word.

In the midst of our growing, we all struggle with our prideful fallen nature and therefore our fallen discernment, which produces a critical spirit and judgmentalism. This side of eternity, even as Christians, we still have a fallen human nature which we can gain the victory over, through our relationship with Jesus and in the power of His Holy Spirit living within us. None of us are perfect but we have a God who is and He is changing us to be like Him. In this we have freedom.

The accuser, the one who condemns and the father of all lies (John 8:44), is the one who will feed our fallen nature and use it against self and others. He will seek to use us if we have a critical spirit to bring condemnation and accusation. Remember that Satan wants what belongs to God. He wants God's place as Judge and is more than able to deceive us into believing he is God. Satan is a master of disguise. Discerning how he operates and works is essential if we are to live in the unity Jesus asked His Father for in John 17:21, *'that they may all be one. As you Father are in me and I am in you, may they also be in us so that the world may believe that you have sent me.'*

There is a real danger that we believe every seemingly good idea, thought or manifestation is coming from God and receive it as such. We then add the weight of our prayers to this belief. The enemy delights in this and will have us agreeing to go down a wrong track. This will ultimately lead us into confusion, into guidance which is not God's way, or even to disillusionment and away from our relationship with Him.

We could find ourselves continuing merrily along, thinking and believing we are doing the right thing but along the way we have left God behind. In so doing, we have grieved the Holy Spirit and we are living out our own desires in God's name but without His presence with us.

Although we are told not to judge men's hearts, we are told to test all things. Weighing, testing and discerning should be paramount if we are to put safety around our own lives and the lives of others.

There are three areas which need the gift of discernment and out of which we need the gift of wisdom.

1.   What is demonic spirit?
2.   What is human spirit?
3.   What is Holy Spirit?

Over the years of praying with individuals we have learnt many lessons in the area of discernment. We are so thankful to God that through some very tough situations, He has taught us and opened our spiritual eyes so we could unlock situations through the discerning of spirits. There are many facets in our discerning of situations and we will need wisdom to go alongside it. I will attempt in this chapter to give some practical examples of how discernment has worked and where the principles may also work for other situations.

There have been times of interceding and praying for an individual when we have been aware that there is a blockage. The flow of prayer or the anointing for healing has ceased. This may even manifest itself through the person we are trying to help.

It has been during these situations that I have learnt to pray the most powerful prayers I know! I would often feel insecure, fearful and inadequate during such times. It felt like a personal failure on my part. My thoughts were - maybe I was just not anointed enough or I was not gifted enough or I didn't have a good enough relationship with the Lord or my bible knowledge was too limited.

I know now the enemy wanted to use my weaknesses and he was trying to intimidate me. I would end up berating myself for what I saw as my failure. The Lord is so kind and throughout these times, I'm so grateful that He would keep encouraging me and showing me that despite my inadequacy, He was faithful and He gave me and the team around me encouragement to press through.

As a result I grew in confidence in the Lord and what He was able to do. I also grew in my discernment that the enemy wanted to keep me in this fearful and insecure place and to drain me of my energy and joy in ministry. My own soul power was making me work harder from this insecure place.

Once I had discerned the plan and strategy of the enemy over my life, I began telling him that it was not down to me, or my expertise, or lack of it. I told him Jesus was going to use me and that I was available to Jesus; it wasn't dependent on me.

From this position, I began to pray a powerful prayer like this: "Lord Jesus, I have come today to learn from You and to work with You in setting Joan free. Please show me what it is You are doing, what it is Satan is doing and what it is Joan is doing." In other words, I was asking the Lord for discernment. Originally, I had thought I had to work it all out from my limited training, understanding or spirituality.

Instead of taking up false responsibility in the situation, I began to relax and enjoy learning from the Lord. Rather than it depending on my own self confidence, I began to grow in confidence in the Lord and the way He worked.

The gift of discernment goes alongside the gift of wisdom. *'A wise man's heart discerns the way'* (Ecclesiastes 8:5). God wants to teach us how to discern His ways. He loves us to ask and enquire of Him. The gift will come if we humbly come before Him and ask for discernment and wisdom about how to pray, speak or act in any given situation.

Discerning guidance

God longs to communicate with us and to show us His heart. It's rare that we will hear an audible voice. The way God speaks and communicates with us is more likely to be through an impression, a thought, an idea or a sense of something which we begin to learn is the Holy Spirit at work within us. It could be an impartation of knowledge or direction. In our discerning the Lord's voice, we need to be careful the enemy is not leading us. There are times when the voice of the enemy and God's voice can sound very similar.

In particular this happens when we are seeking guidance. Usually we seek guidance when we are unsettled and uncertain about something. We are in need of an answer and therefore looking for some sign which confirms or denies our direction. At these times, it's important to 'discern' what is going on in our own soul and we will need someone in authority over us or who is mature enough to give a wise answer. It's worth remembering that soul power will cause us to 'listen' to anything which makes our soul feel good and delivers the answer we want, rather than the answer we need.

Having been in Christian leadership for many years now, and sadly I have seen how easy it is for the enemy to direct people according to their soul and yet they are convinced this leading has come from God. You often find that the enemy will direct a person to an 'easy way' out in a difficult situation. Usually this direction is not shared or submitted to anyone who would question or test the guidance but rather with those who are likely to agree to the easier or 'soulish' way.

I have found that a good sign of this is when the person wanting guidance does not seek to weigh and test. They have made up their minds and defend their decision defensively and even ferociously. Once I discern this, I know it is of no avail to begin to shed any different light on their situation. A mind made up is a mind which isn't open to change. The person is simply looking for affirmation rather than godly impartation.

We have seen some people miss God's best way because Satan has managed to appeal to their soul in the name of God and effectively deceive them. We need the gift of discerning of spirits along with the gift of wisdom and we need to seek out those who are mature for help in order to test whether something has truly come from God or not. It's in the area of guidance that we can move out of the best place God has for us if we have not been willing to fully submit and hear from others who exercise discernment, as well as use our own discernment.

It's extremely easy to be deceived and as Derek Prince once said, "if you think you can't be deceived, you already are!" *'The heart is deceitful above all things'* (Jeremiah 17:9). Being under godly authority is the best way to avoid being deceived. Our hearts do deceive us and this isn't just a once in a lifetime experience. This is why we need those who speak into our lives with godly confrontation as well as affirmation ('faithful are the wounds of a friend' Proverbs 27:6).

It's so easy for us to use God's authority to give 'soulish' advice and guidance. Our human nature wants to make everything easy, comfortable and kind. We need to be sure before we say anything to someone seeking help, guidance or direction that we have sought the Lord's wisdom and discernment.

Conversely, we need to be extremely careful in the way we ourselves hear the Lord. When we have been hurt and betrayed, we find it hard to trust another. From this position, it's very easy to walk in independence. We can become loners and become those who hear God for our own selves rather than through anybody else.

We regularly meet people who tell us what God has said to them and how He has directed them. Their expectation is that we will be pleased and we will agree. Wisdom has taught us to test and weigh (discern) the way a person has made the decision and has come to their conclusion. It's not always easy to be in a leadership position because you can't always agree and say the nice things people want you to say and give the look of pleasure they want you to give.

In these situations where the discernment is that the person has not heard the Lord and has made their decision out of their 'soulish' desire and more importantly, has not submitted their decision in the right way, we have to be extremely careful how we pray. We can't put our agreement in prayer to something which comes out of human thinking. If we did so, we would be giving spiritual power to what we believe to be a deception.

Discerning prayer will ask the Lord to lead and guide the person according to His purposes. It will ask the Lord to bless the person in their future life but it can't give a 'thank You' to the Lord for the way He is leading and guiding!

Discerning criticism

A breakthrough came about one day in a ministry with a particular lady who was terribly broken. Her background was one where she had been completely rubbished by her own family. As a result she had absolutely no self esteem or worth. She believed she was born 'bad.' Satan had done his work in her life and had well and truly bound her up in the belief that what had happened to her was because she was bad. I remember an occasion when we were helping and teaching her to enjoy herself and express her creativity. Hitherto she had been unable to enter into any freedom to do so.

While we were adventuring and playing with paints, shapes and ideas with paper on the floor, this lady made what she saw as a mistake in what she was doing. She tore it up believing it all to be bad and rubbish just because of one mistake. We were able to help her see that God did not see her or what she had made that way. God saw the journey she was taking. He saw her choose the colors, He enjoyed being with her as she experimented and as she received her ideas. He loved her and He loved what she was making.

God's love for her was not dependent on what she was creating and how good or perfect it was. His love and pleasure was in seeing her being herself and free to explore and grow. There is no one on the planet who arrives anywhere without experimenting, exploring, and therefore growing in a gift. One day I hope to write a book on 'Healing through Creativity' which is one of the areas through which the Lord has brought profound and deep healing to many.

As we progress with the gift of discernment, we will need to identify the difference between criticism which is fallen, and the beauty of discernment which is in essence through God's eyes. We will also need to learn how to discern spiritual matters, not just issues of the physical realm.

Seeing things through God's eyes doesn't mean we become sentimental and accepting of everything but 'through His eyes' means we see things positively for change and growth. The frustration we go through will be turned into a motivating force by the Holy Spirit. The condemnation we receive will change to become a conviction against the work of the enemy and will place us back into the center of God's plan. He wants to teach us to change and grow through these circumstances.

The lady in the illustration learnt a profound lesson. She learnt that when she ripped up her efforts and put them in a bin in disgust, she was in effect ripping herself up in disgust. She was exercising self loathing and hatred, a putting away of herself and the precious person she was to us and to God. The enemy was smugly enjoying it and encouraging her along. When we shared these truths with her, her spirit opened up to receive the truth and from that time on she began to grow steadfastly in her acceptance of herself and confidence in God. Her amazing creative gifting flowed and this in itself spoke to her of how good God is and of her worth to Him.

Discerning the human spirit

I remember being in a ministry situation where we were getting nowhere. The ministry team with me were desperately trying to find the key to unlock the impasse in the person's life and no matter how hard they tried there was no response. They then began to battle against the enemy thinking that this must be the problem.

At this time I prayed for the gift of discernment. Almost immediately a thought came into my mind to ask the lady in question whether she was comfortable. I had a strong sense that she was not. She went on to explain that she didn't like sitting in the seat she was on because she felt trapped. It turned out that having been sexually abused as a child she became panic stricken when she was not near a door to escape if she needed to. Once we had resolved this problem and changed the seating arrangement, the ministry flowed.

The answer to prayer in this situation came as we discerned that the problem was locked in the person's human spirit. The lady was full of insecurity and fear, and the block on that day was resolved simply. I learnt that at times the Lord uses our common sense discernment in many ministry situations.

During other very deep ministry situations, the person we have been helping has spoken out significant words and feelings which are coming from the flesh (or the soul). We have been able to discern that behind these words or feelings is a human sense of rejection or failure, a desire to give up, to reject us or to project blame to someone else. There is often the desire to escape, or to orchestrate an agenda which is not God's agenda.

When the human spirit is crushed and damaged, the person finds it extremely difficult to rise up in any faith or belief that anything can change. Discerning this is crucial in order to be effective in helping the person engage in the plans and purposes of God for them and their destiny. It's here that intercession is needed to discern where the crushing lies and from there to move on in prayer to strengthen the person and see them grow under the hand of the Lord.

The person may be projecting feelings such as overwhelm, guilt, discomfort, distress, mistrust, worthlessness, abandonment or injustice from past hurt into the present circumstances. We have to discern this. We must learn how to bring healing and comfort from the Lord into such areas. Discernment is not just to do with discerning the enemy.

Common sense discernment

During another troublesome ministry time, I was confronted by a man who was extremely drunk and rebellious. None of the men on our ministry team were able to calm the situation when this man refused to move from the place he was occupying on the roof outside.

The ministry team were binding demonic spirits or commanding them to leave. However, the Lord does not give us authority over anyone's free will and in this situation the man was not co-operating with us and therefore the demons certainly weren't either!

I was asked to help and I found myself asking the Lord what I should do or say. Out of my mouth came the words, "I'm cold waiting out here for you; for goodness sake, come inside." Like a lamb the man walked in! The Lord had given me very ordinary discernment and wisdom in what to say and do. I understood that day that the way God leads us sometimes is seemingly not spiritual at all. He is the God of plain common, practical sense!

Common sense discernment can be exercised in many ways. Sometimes the person is simply not ready for spiritual interaction. They don't want to do business with the Lord. Discerning the timing is an all-important lesson. As compassionate people, we sometimes desire to fix it, to make everything comfortable and nice!

The person may be sobbing deeply and we bring along a tissue to help them dry their eyes! However, the Lord is doing His work through their sobbing and their relationship with Him at this point is intimate and precious. We need discernment to know when to intervene with human comfort.

However, at another time a person may be sobbing and simply need the common sense discernment which brings the cup of tea and a friendly chat. The enemy sometimes wants to keep people in distressed conditions and feeds on this.

We can sometimes stir the enemy up by spiritualizing every-thing and making what is human and normal into a spiritual battle. It's as if the enemy says, "Alright, you want a battle, we will give you one." Before we know it, we are being drawn into something which the enemy can use to escalate and take up hours of our time and much heartache in relationship.

We have to remember that some people find it easier to enter into a spiritual battle than to face the real and practical issues of their life. It's not easy to face up to inadequacy, failure, loss and so on.

In these cases, we need to discern whether to look at the situa-tion through common sense or enter into a spiritual battle.

Before we engage in battles we need to ask the Lord the ques-tion, "what is going on here?" and ask Him to give us His wisdom and discernment. There have been other times when we were ministering when it seemed as though the person was being so spiritually minded and heightened that he or she almost lost the sense of being a human being. This isn't healthy. The human spirit and soul need human relationship and contact. If there are times when this is lost, then I believe the person needs help to engage in ordinary human life, communication and activity.

It's necessary to have a balanced view. It's possible to put everything down to common sense and rationalize or to go to the other extreme and see everything as spiritual. In order to be 'naturally' supernatural we need to walk in both these areas of discernment.

Discerning the enemy

There are many ways the enemy works. Demonic spirits only enter people when they have rights to do so. Peter's book 'Healing through Deliverance' is a thorough work on this subject so I don't intend repeating the teaching here. However in our intercessory role, we will need to, *'smell the enemy'*. By this I mean to get to know his character.

The bible describes Satan as the father of lies, the accuser and the condemner. We can exercise discernment by 'smelling' these traits in the relationships and situations we find ourselves in. If we see manipulation and twisting of truth, we know who is behind this. If we see accusation and malicious intent, we will know who is behind it. If we receive or hear unforgiving judgmentalism, we will know who is behind that.

The enemy seeks to counterfeit that which God conceived and to twist it. He is a robber and if he can't rob us, he will seek to take that which belongs to us out of balance and into his hands. He would try to steal what belongs to God for his own glory. We need great discernment to see the work of the enemy and to be guarded against it.

Division is another trait of the enemy. He attempts to set one off against another, using human weakness in the process and then delights in the pain and distress the division has caused.

The taking of offence is another typical footprint the enemy leaves behind. A book by John Bevere entitled 'The Bait of Satan' is excellent on this subject. There is a right offense that Jesus caused when He came up against the religious rulers of the day. As a result of the kingdom of God being established here on earth through the reign of Jesus, we will cause a right and godly offense. However, the ungodly offenses will come when we pick up on a behavior, a disagreement or a characteristic which affronts us. When we walk with offense, we will pass this on to another person and influence them and the end result will be walking in bitterness. The enemy will use this to bring division.

A man came for help who was tremendously gifted musically. Deep down inside this man was broken. He had come from a home where his father was an alcoholic. His mother spent all her energy attempting to keep the home perfect so that there would be no outbursts from her easily angered husband.

In a subconscious way the mother was injecting fear into her children who hardly dared move in case they were the cause of their father's alcoholic binges. The man who came for help had memories of severe beatings and as a consequence he was unable to express his gifting. When we prayed for him, the injustice and anger inside bubbled to the surface. The man immediately shut down his emotions. He was too frightened to allow anything to be out of control.

At this point the enemy was cruelly accusing him of his failure and inadequacy as a child and how he had not met his father's expectations. The enemy had piled blame and false guilt onto the man as a boy and was now compounding this as an adult.

Finally, we were able to help him see that Jesus wanted him to be real and to let out the mess on the inside of him. The anger and injustice came pouring out. Much of it was the man's genuine emotions but the enemy was using them. Satan had an inroad through the trauma and fear the man had experienced as a boy. As a ministry team we needed discernment to see that the enemy was operating on this man's broken-ness and producing an anger and venom far outweighing the natural anger that was there.

The enemy had a stronghold in which he wanted this man to continue to take the blame and guilt for this anger. We could discern there was a stronghold there which was not coming from the man himself. Jesus gloriously delivered the man and he was able to pour out his real and natural anger and injustice to the Lord with holy tears and with joy that his Heavenly Father loved him so much.

The characteristic of the enemy is that he will come with the extreme and with the deception that it is impossible to heal or to be free.

Discerning the Holy Spirit in action

While looking at the discerning of the human spirit, it's also important for us to see that the Lord speaks through the human spirit too. In the dialogue Jesus has with Simon Peter in Matthew 16:13-17, we can see this very clearly. Jesus said, *"But who do you say that I am?"* Simon Peter answered, *"You are the Messiah, the Son of the Living God."* And Jesus answered him, *"Blessed are you, Simon son of Jonah! For flesh and blood has not revealed this to you, but my Father in heaven."*

In exercising discernment, it's helpful to ask the Holy Spirit to show us when a person we are helping is speaking something out which is from God. I have learnt to listen for a conviction to rise up within the person I am praying for, which is coming out of their human spirit but is in fact the Holy Spirit's work within them. At these times, it is important that we pick this up in prayer and speak out our agreement and "amen."

Words of conviction such as "I really am not a failure" or "God does love me" or "I will be safe, Jesus is with me," are a sign of the Holy Spirit witnessing truth in the innermost parts.

Sometimes these words of conviction come in the form of questions such as such as, "do you believe me?" or "is this really true?" or "is God going to use me?" In listening carefully, we can learn to discern that the Holy Spirit is prompting the question and the Holy Spirit is requiring our Holy Spirit led response in order to confirm and seal in a precious truth.

The Lord wants to reveal to us what His Holy Spirit is doing and for us to recognize the Holy Spirit's guiding and power within the person we are helping. The Holy Spirit will bring to the surface (if the person is willing) an attitude, behavior, belief or mood which will help us in our discerning of the situation.

Conversely, if the person is not willing then the Holy Spirit will show us that there is no openness for the power of God to move in the life of that person or in that situation. If this is the case, then all we can do is to pray for God's right timing or for Him to break down the walls of opposition. We can also pray that any plan of the enemy is broken over the situation or the person's life. However, until the time is right, we can't be involved further.

The enemy would love us to waste time and effort when a person's will is not open to the Lord and may even be in rebellion towards Him. There are some things we need to leave to the Lord's timing. There may well be other things the Lord wants to do in a given circumstance or person. We need discernment and wisdom to know if the human spirit is not co-operating with the Holy Spirit.

Additional Practical Prayers and Points

The prayer of desperation

When we come to the end of ourselves, it is the beginning of God! The best prayer we can pray is the prayer of desperation! When I spoke about this prayer at one of our conferences everyone broke into laughter. They knew exactly what I was talking about – the "Oh God help!" prayer!

The truth is that we all know this prayer. We say the words, "Oh God help" in many situations where we don't have the answers and there is no time for prolonged prayer either. However, I am talking here about a deeper prayer of desperation. It is when we have truly reached rock bottom, we have no way out and if God doesn't hear us, disaster could be upon us. Even those in the world pray this when they are truly up against it, such as in an aircraft about to crash.

From this place, there is a gut wrenching cry which comes from within. There is nothing else to do but place oneself wholly at the mercy of Almighty God. Our loving heavenly Father loves these cries because it is here that He can truly come to us and either deliver us or uphold us and give us His peace and strength.

It's interesting that when we are really up against it, we turn to the Psalms for comfort and we identify with the Scripture. King David in the Psalms knew exactly how to be real with God. His intercession was not false. He didn't offer up to God passive platitudes but rather, out of the depth of his being, he let his feelings be known.

In Psalm 69:1-3, King David cried out to the Lord, *"save me, O God, for the waters have come up to my neck. I sink in deep mire, where there is no foothold; I have come into deep waters and the flood sweeps over me. I am weary with my crying; my throat is parched. My eyes grow dim waiting for my God"*. David expressed every emotion he had in this Psalm.

It's when we are real with God that He can then come and intervene on our behalf. We have witnessed this on countless occasions whilst praying with people. It seems that whilst their defenses are up or while they are finding ways to fix the situation themselves, God can't bring his solution. There is something about coming to the end of ourselves that moves the heart of God into action. So, we should not be afraid of allowing a person to come to the end of themselves and should be careful not to intervene in the process because God will be at work.

Earlier in the book, I told the story of the siege and how as a ministry we had come to the end of the road financially. In desperation, we cried out to God to save us and in a miraculous way, He did! We can't engineer these situations but when we find ourselves in them, we can be sure that God is very close and He hears our cry to Him. He is not passively sitting by without any action.

I have found over the years that I welcome the reality of this prayer in people's lives. Passivity, complacency and comfort are enemies to effectiveness in intercession. It's when I have witnessed someone on their knees pleading with God to help, that I know He will!

From a healing perspective, there are times when you touch broken-ness in people because of the trauma and pain of their past. Man's inhumanity to man has taken its toll and the people we are praying for are broken as a result. At these times the compassion of the Lord Jesus wells up within our hearts to bring His comfort, His grace, mercy and healing.

There are also times when the breaking is what God is doing. We witness the Lord breaking pride, rebellion or the stubborn rejection of His way. This will be a precious and holy time when we see people desperate for God to change them. This kind of prayer of desperation is when true repentance is taking place and as those who stand alongside, we should take care to allow the Holy Spirit to do whatever work He needs to do.

In intercession it's necessary for us to know the difference between the breaking and desperation which comes through circumstances and pain versus the breaking which God brings through the conviction of sin. Both produce desperation and both cries are very precious and holy to the Lord.

Prayer of 'having done all else – stand'

There are times in our reaching out to others when we come to an end of what we are able to do. We may be lost for words. We can't fix the situation or make it okay. Conversely for the person receiving, they may have come to the end of what they can take.

It's often at this point that the enemy is particularly close. He loves to taunt us, point out seeming failure or our inability to change a situation. Over the years it has been hard when walking with the deeply broken to see them struggle and sometimes suffer because there is not an obvious answer or way forward.

It has been at these times, I have learnt to exercise the prayer of "having done all else to stand." In Exodus chapter 14, Moses found himself in the same situation. In verse 13 of the chapter it says, *'Moses said to the people, "Do not be afraid, stand firm, and see the deliverance that the Lord will accomplish for you today. The Lord will fight for you, and you have only to keep still".*

Sometimes, there is nothing else to do but to stand still. I encourage people that they are on a mountain climb and have climbed so far. Yes, there is still a way to go but we aren't going to let the enemy rob them of the journey they have taken already. There is a place for establishing the ground which has been taken and holding fast to it. It can be useful and faith-building for an individual if we explain that we may not be able to go on further yet, but neither are we taking any steps backwards.

We can encourage an individual in how well they have done in their walk so far and that now is the time to stand firm. Ephesians

6 verse 13 says '*and having done everything, to stand firm.*' We place a stake in the ground and declare that this is where we are and we are not going to go up or down but for the time being we will stand firm.

Encouragement is needed when we can't see an answer especially following much battle. In 2 Chronicles 20:17, Jehoshaphat's prayer was answered by the Lord with, '*This battle is not for you to fight; take your position, stand still and see the victory of the Lord on your behalf*'.

It's sometimes in the standing and waiting that we will see God do His most powerful work. This is not necessarily a comfortable place to be, as it requires trust. God is outside of time and His timing is not like ours. He knows things we don't and holds a greater plan for victory than we can imagine.

Prayer of quietness and/or silence

Psalm 62:1 -2 says '*For God alone my soul waits in silence; from Him comes my salvation; He alone is my rock and my salvation, my fortress; I shall never be shaken.*'

We shouldn't be afraid of silence. Sometimes people are so used to the tumult this world brings that silence causes them to panic. We have been programmed to expect action and when neither action nor words take place, it can make some people very insecure. However, it's in the silence that God will speak.

He will wait until we have emptied ourselves of our talk and of our thoughts and come to the place where we are yielded before Him and ready to wait on Him and to listen. His holiness comes in the silence and it's strengthening to our spirits and souls.

In the work of healing, there is often much deep emotion being expressed or there is the noise of battle as the enemy is uprooted. I have found that immediately following these times, it's good to wait in silence. People receiving help have engaged deeply with the Lord and now their soul is to be quieted in His presence. It's here we have experienced remarkable times of the Lord speaking uniquely and profoundly into their life.

Prayer of tongues

The gift of tongues comes when we let go of our own control to form words and allow the Holy Spirit to form them, 1 Corinthians 14:13-14. It's not something that takes us over but rather a receiving from the Lord of His gift. It's a precious gift in intercession.

There are many times when I have found that I'm lost for words. I have simply come to an end of what I can think or know to pray or say. I remember a time when the situation we were involved in was locked in an awkward silence as opposed to a holy silence. I had a sense that whatever any of us said, the enemy was waiting to use it in a wrong way. The person we were praying for was heightened in her anger and injustice and the demonic behind it was fuelling this and making ready to cause havoc both with her and us.

The only prayer we could pray was the prayer of tongues. To begin with this was done quietly and then more boldly. The demonic power was disarmed and revealed itself shouting, "Shut up, shut up." The demons know that speaking in tongues is a powerful weapon against them as it brings the anointing of the Holy Spirit which breaks the yoke. Praying in tongues is a spiritual warfare weapon.

This prayer is not only for battling situations. It can be used when we want to come before the Lord for His guidance or help. Allowing the prayer of tongues to flow through us shows a yielded heart to the Lord and He releases the anointing of His Holy Spirit. When we are praying in tongues, we are receiving the mind of the Lord. I have found on countless occasions that I have then had the words to say and wisdom on the way forward.

The interpretation of the gift of tongues doesn't necessarily flow as a word for word type of sentence. It can come in the form of an impression, a thought or a flow of words which are Holy Spirit inspired, filled with wisdom and discernment. They may also hold an element of prophetic exhortation, forth telling the word of the Lord.

There is no set pattern for praying in tongues. Sometimes it's good to begin your prayer time in tongues as this will release your spirit from the clutter of the day. Intercession will then flow readily. At other times, praying in tongues comes naturally during a time of praise and worship and brings a release to our spirit which will rise in faith and trust in the Lord as a result. Following prayer in our natural language, the gift of tongues will flow as we have touched the heart of God and He is touching us.

It is the language of heaven and with it comes the sweet presence of the Lord. The enemy does not like it as it disarms him but the angels rejoice because it empowers them to do God's work at His bidding.

Prayer of sealing

2 Corinthians 1:20-22 says, *'For in him every one of God's promises is a 'Yes'. For this reason it is through Him that we say the 'Amen', to the glory of God. But it is God who establishes us with you in Christ and has anointed us, by putting his seal on us and giving us his Spirit in our hearts as a first installment.'*

When we speak out an "amen" we are saying, "so let it be." We are taking our position in Christ Jesus and making a powerful agreement to God's promises. God in turn seals his promise to us through the Holy Spirit.

At certain times in praying for people, we have found it particularly meaningful and powerful to ask the Lord to seal into the person everything which is of Him and especially to keep sealed that which has been committed to Him. The Lord and the person are not the only ones who hear this prayer.

During prayer ministry, many things will have been prayed through and accomplished in the heavenly realms. It will be impossible for the person to remember everything and yet they want to do so, for fear of losing what God has done. Praying that the Lord would put a seal around all that has been accomplished in His name, both encourages the person and it gives the enemy notice that nothing can be stolen by him.

Anointing prayer

The use of oil as a sign of anointing is quite common throughout Scripture. In 1 Samuel 16:1- 3 we read that the Lord told Samuel to take anointing oil and to anoint King David. Here we have an example of anointing prayer for a specific purpose and task.

Whenever we appoint a leader or a welcome a new team member, we have found it a very holy and special time as we have anointed them with oil in the name of the Father, Son and Holy Spirit and set them apart for the calling and service they are about to enter.

In James 5:14, we are told to pray over the person who is sick and anoint them with oil. We have certainly experienced the supernatural power of God at work many times when we have followed this injunction. Our work involves praying for many who have experienced severe trauma. As a result of trauma, people often suffer physical sickness and even disability. Following the prayer for inner healing and deliverance, we then go on to ask the Lord to bring physical healing. It's then that we have taken oil, prayed over the oil and anointed the person, inviting the Lord to come and heal and as a result we have witnessed many dramatic physical healings.

Physical healing is not the only healing we can receive in Jesus' name. A woman came to us for prayer who was severely demonized. She had been involved in the occult and as a result had battled greatly to keep her life on track since she had become a Christian. The undelivered powers within her had so many rights that they dragged her into old ways and behaviors which left her desperate.

When we came to bring her freedom in the name of Jesus through being delivered, the powers within her didn't go quietly and the battles continued until we ran out of energy. We were left wondering how this could be when it was obvious to us that Jesus had won the victory and yet it wasn't being evidenced. It later emerged that the whole family had an occult history which meant that she herself had been involved since childhood. Oaths and pacts had been made on her behalf.

It was through this and similar experiences with other people, that we learnt the power of the sacraments. In giving communion, for example, if we didn't pray over the bread and the wine, things appeared normal. But, when we did pray and ask the Lord to bless the elements and fill them with His Holy Spirit for the purpose of communion that day, it made a difference!

We found that the demonic inside the person would rise up and try to get her to run out of the room! Demons would even attempt to seal her lips so tightly, they were unable to take of the elements. With the person's will engaging rightly, we experienced powerful deliverances following the taking of communion.

During such spiritual battles, it emerged that the powers of darkness hated an outward sign of an inward truth. As a result we began to pray for each person coming to us for deep deliverance, anointing them beforehand with oil. We also anointed the ministry team for their part in God's purposes that day. It's a powerful tool for the release of the anointing of God and establishing authority over the powers of darkness.

In Exodus 40:9-11, we learn that anointing oil was used to consecrate the temple buildings to make them holy and also everything within them, which were to be set apart for holy purposes. We are the temples of the Holy Spirit and as such we need to take care that those things we own and have authority over are spiritually clean.

Demons will indwell buildings, places, possessions and objects if they have rights to do so. For instance, we have learnt to pray in the hotel rooms we stay in. Often when entering, we discern the heavy, repelling oppression of a spiritual power which is unclean. This isn't surprising, since most hotel rooms are occupied by a variety of people who may be involved in the occult, false religions, dishonest practices, unclean sexuality (especially pornography) and blasphemy. Once we have prayed, cleansed and anointed the room, the difference in the atmosphere is like night and day. We are immediately able to feel comfortable and to pray and relax. I would highly recommend Christians to do that.

Gifts are another example. Gifts that have been given with good intent but where you have no awareness of where they come from, such as antiques, heirlooms, second hand jewelry and the like, may have power attached to them from a previous owner. When we have traveled in places like South Africa for example, we have been very aware that some of the craft stalls have powerfully demonic objects for sale which tourists buy unwittingly without realizing the danger behind their purchase.

I was once traveling abroad and shopped in what seemed like a very clean mall. I had visited many of the shops along the way and was thoroughly enjoying the culture and array of goods for sale. However, in one particular shop just as I was about to purchase some postcards, I began to feel ill. I wanted to get out of the shop. As I looked up I saw a whole wall full of the most horrible masks. I had encountered many shops with masks but this shop was different.

The postcards were put back on the shelf as I left the shop quickly. My friend was waiting for me to join her in the Christian bookshop opposite. As I entered the bookshop, my chest began to tighten and wheeze! The onset of this was so sudden, it was unbelievable. I immediately knew the Lord was showing me that although many shops may have some element of occult, false religion or idolatrous objects, the one I had entered was particularly dangerous because the owners practiced the occult. The one I had visited was extremely dark in this regard.

I knew how to pray and asked the Lord to cut any tie between me and the shop. In an instant, I was set free from the oppression which had attached itself to me and the wheezing ceased.

There have been times when we have been taking conferences outside of our centers and have been allotted community halls or places where there have been many different kinds of practices. I remember on one occasion we found that our conference was being slotted in between the activities of a psychic fair! You can imagine that we wondered how we would be able to bring God's Word and anointing for healing and deliverance in the midst of this.

We have learnt to pray over oil asking the Lord to anoint it and bless it in the name of the Father, Son and Holy Spirit. When we have used the anointing oil in this way and prayed over objects, buildings or possessions in order to set them free from any curses or demonic strongholds which could affect us, we have experienced powerful results.

Caution should be exercised here not to become legalistic or superstitious. The enemy wants to take us to extremes whereby we become fearful or paranoid if we have not done exactly the right thing, said the right prayer and discerned the precise demon. The Lord is full of love and grace towards us. He wants us to be aware of dark spiritual power but not walk in fear of it. It is His desire to teach us and open our eyes to the tools He has provided but not for us to use them like a piece of magic. Our safety is in trusting Him to open our spiritual eyes of discernment and to teach us if there is anything deeply wrong.

Practical points

To conclude this chapter, I am adding some practical points which I pray will be of help to you in your adventure in intercession.

1. Self consciousness and human inhibition can be a great stumbling block in prayer. I grew up with the 'hands together, eyes shut' model. In later years, through the work of healing, I discovered it was a good idea to keep your eyes open whilst praying as all sorts of things could be happening around you. There was once a time when we were all praying fervently and when we opened our eyes, the person we were praying for had left the room!

It is good to watch and pray! It is in the watching that you see emotion or possibly distraction. You can begin to asses the response and discern what to pray or whether to stop praying altogether! It is easy to go into a lengthy engagement of prayer which you are enjoying but has left everyone else behind or more importantly the person you are attempting to help.

I will be forever grateful to some early teachers who came to Ellel to help us understand prayer and intercession as well as spiritual warfare. It was then that I began to let go of my self consciousness and enter into effective praying. We were taught to speak out loud the names and characteristics of God in a corporate setting. I found this tremendously difficult at first but persevered until there came a time when I was totally free in my outward expression to God of who He is, and could enter into intercession with a love and passion which welled up from within me.

This kind of praying both in a large corporate meeting or in a small one with just one or two people present will touch the heart of God. I also learnt that alongside corporately speaking out who God is, that I needed to speak out declarations which put the enemy firmly in his place. He hates it when we declare loudly and openly that Jesus is Lord and that we have the victory in His name!

Our personal inhibitions can become an obstacle to the way the Lord wants to use us and it is a good prayer to ask Him to help us launch out in faith in this respect. With perseverance, it will become more natural to us.

2. Along with our self consciousness, come our normal human feelings. Being engaged in spiritual activity can be very tiring. It is easy to become tired and irritable. I have experienced times when I have even fallen asleep!

On the other hand, we could find ourselves becoming fed up or bored. We may become distracted and disinterested. It isn't easy for our humanity to keep going with long sessions. This is normal. However, I have found there are times when there is a need to push through my human feelings and persevere! As a result I have been rewarded with a breakthrough.

At other times, it's important to know the right time to draw to a close. If the enemy can't stop us being used spiritually, he will try to get us to be over-spiritual. We are human and have human needs which are an important factor in intercession. God didn't make us divine nor did He make us angels. There are times when He calls us to sacrifice our time and needs, but not all the time and He knows we need a balance in order to be refreshed and renewed.

3. Our Heavenly Father wants to pour things back into us. He likes to surprise us with His love and to give us His joy! His joy is our strength! Isaiah 58 speaks of how the Lord will cause our

own healing to spring up quickly as we serve the needs of others. We don't serve out of a motivation to gain but out of love for our Lord. However, the truth is that when our motivation is out of love and service for Jesus, He in turn gives back more than we could ever give to Him!

I have lost count of the occasions when God has rewarded me personally and very deeply. He has heard my cry and met my needs. I am constantly amazed at the way He has kept me strong and healthy and given me renewed strength. In fact, there are times when I just don't know where the energy flows from as I have never been a naturally energetic person!

The promise in Isaiah 40:31 will come to pass, '*but those who wait for the Lord shall renew their strength, they shall mount up with wings like eagles, they shall run and not be weary, they shall walk and not faint.*' This is our inheritance as sons and daughters of the King.

The story of Ellel Ministries is one of the Lord constantly providing and supplying our needs in extraordinary and wonderful ways. God is our Provider. These things may not come in the same way as when we go to the supermarket, where our food comes home neatly packaged and in parcels. God provides for us in a variety of ways which are beyond our imagination. He wants our eyes to be opened up to His provision and to trust Him for it.

As sons and daughters of the King, we can live rich and fulfilling lives. We are not dependent on outward circumstances but rather on our Heavenly Father who pours out His grace, enabling and strengthening in times of need and gives us His joy in serving Him. It's the kind of joy response which defies logic and wells up in spite of us. It's the same with provision. We may be poor but we are rich and we may be weak but we are strong. We are invited to live in God's kingdom which turns the world's value system on its head.

The Intercessory Goal – the Prayer of Jesus to His Father

'That they may be one.'

John chapter 17:22 (NRSV)

The Lord Jesus is our divine representative before the Father. He is our Intercessor and *'He ever lives to make intercession for us'* (Hebrews 7:25). No matter what our circumstances are, we are not alone. Jesus Himself is lifting us up before the throne of His Father praying for us. He is beseeching His Father on our behalf to protect us from the world we live in because He knows we don't belong to this world. We are called out of this world, to be in it but not of it.

Jesus knew how hard this would be for us and that we would come under all manner of pressures, attacks and hatred because we belong to Him. The intercessory burden placed on Jesus was to ask His Father to protect us from the evil one. He had full knowledge of the character of Satan. He knows the enemy is the father of lies, a thief and out to bring destruction.

Jesus prayed to His Father (John17:17) for our sanctification in the truth, which is His Word. He knew that only by abiding in His Word would we be safe. Sanctification can sound like an old fashioned word but it describes the change which takes place within us as we grow in our walk with Jesus, applying His living Word which is truth and life.

His Holy Spirit within will bring conviction of sin and give us the desire to change our attitudes. We will see circumstances and situations from His perspective rather than from our limited human perspective. It's a divine heart transplant – receiving a heart of flesh instead of a heart of stone. God intends that this will be our place of joy and fulfillment. It will bring safety and protection and bear great fruit in our lives.

As we trust Him with our lives, He will bring about our own individual intercessory calling. This isn't designed to be an appendage in our relationship with Jesus. Rather it's meant to be a part of who we are in Him. Our intercession will be uniquely designed and outworked in each of us according to our own personhood, gifting and calling. Jesus the Great Intercessor is part of us and we are part of Him. The work of the Holy Spirit within us will be changing us from within, to bring forth much fruit for His kingdom.

God made each of us distinct and unique. He has designed a human and God shaped niche for each of us to fit in perfectly. When we belong to Him, He takes our own individual journey and makes sense of it. He redeems those things that have been damaged, broken or lost and in His infinite love and tenderness gives them true value. There is nothing any one of us can go through that is lost to Jesus. Our Heavenly Father turns the desert into living streams and gives back the years the locusts have eaten (Joel 2:25).

It has been the most humbling and precious part of my Christian life to experience our amazing Creator God, the master craftsman, at work bringing about His powerful redemption to those who are crushed in spirit, in deep despair and broken-hearted.

There is nowhere else where the heart of God beats more strongly for us than the place of oppression and injustice. It is here, when invited, He does His most magnificent work. Where there is suffering and pain we can reach out in our relationship with Jesus for His Holy Spirit to come and bring comfort. God is the God of all comfort and strength.

He feels and knows our struggles and pain and His heart at these times is very close to us. Isaiah 53:3 tells us that Jesus was a man of suffering and acquainted with infirmity. Our tears matter to the heart of God. He doesn't invalidate our pain but rather gives place to our suffering and pain. Psalm 56:8-9 says, '*You have kept count of my tossings and put my tears in your bottle.*'

We see in John chapter 17, the heart of Jesus in intercession for us who belong to Him. Jesus is saying, "*As you, Father, are in me and I am in you, may they also be in us, so that the world may believe that you have sent me. The glory that you have given me I have given them, so that they may be one, as we are one. I in them and you in me, that they may become completely one, so that the world may know that you have sent me and have loved them even as you have loved me*". John 17:21-24

What is God's glory? The glory is when we are in Him and He is in us and we become one with Him and one with each other. There is no greater glory than this. Jesus earnestly interceded for this before His Father. The goal is that we may be so one with God, sensing His heart for the lost and broken, that we ourselves become an expression of His character and nature to others. In this way, we become one together.

Our unity is not based on our opinions, personalities, culture or upbringings, but is based on the place which levels each of us – our need of the cross of Jesus where He paid the price for us to receive forgiveness, mercy and grace. This was His ultimate act of intercession, where He willingly sacrificed His life in order that we could receive His life and where our need of Him is met.

When, with one heart and voice, we express the nature and character of our Lord Jesus, in gratitude for His great love for us, and flowing out from that comes our love for Him and for each other, then we will see the glory of God. We will see the blessing of God flow and the powers of darkness put to flight. We will become participators with Him in the glory.

Our Father in Heaven longs to pour out His love and to draw to Himself all who want to receive it. He has chosen those who belong to Him to be channels of that love and mercy.

I pray this book is an encouragement for you to enter into your own intercessory calling, however small you may think it is. Remember God is the one who gives the multiplication. We are called to sow and He will bring in the harvest in due time.

Whatever we give to the Lord never goes unseen, nor is it disregarded. His desire is to turn our lives into fruitful gardens. One day when we meet Him face to face, we will see the full picture and how those things given sacrificially to Him have mattered and been multiplied.

Our intercession is *'storing up treasure in heaven where neither moth nor rust consumes and where thieves do not break in and steal'* (Matthew 6:20).

Sometimes we will see the answers to our prayers and the fruit of our intercession and at other times it may remain hidden for some time or even never be known to us in this life.

Finally, whatever, our part is, as we walk this incredible journey with our loving Heavenly Father, we should always remember to give Him all the glory for what He has done.

May the Lord Jesus bless you as you step out in your journey and your life of fruitfulness in His kingdom.

Finally, for your encouragement:-

The little blue flower

As a little girl growing up, I loved to hear true stories. My Auntie Winnie who is now with the Lord, having passed away at the ripe old age of 98, was a wealth of wonderful stories of how the Lord worked in her life and I loved to hear them. She was a true woman of faith and led a life of great fruitfulness for God.

Auntie Win's husband was a bank manager who retired early from his job in the north of England and they moved to Cornwall. Uncle Nick wanted to buy a farm and I have wonderful memories of staying there as a child and enjoying the cream which came from their beautiful herd of Jersey cows.

At their home in the north of England a little rock plant with blue flowers grew and blossomed well. Auntie Winnie told me that she had loved this plant and when they moved to Cornwall, she took cuttings from it. She remembered praying, "O Lord, please make this little blue flower grow here in Cornwall, I love it so much and it reminds me of home."

Sadly, it did not appear the following year. Auntie Winnie thought it had died and was so disappointed. The plant had meant a great deal to her.

A staggering fourteen years later, she woke one morning to see patches of blue between some cobbles in the farmyard! As the days wore on the farmyard became absolutely ablaze with blue! The little plant had somehow survived, gone underground and all those years later had found its own way to blossom!

As Auntie Winnie was rejoicing, she felt the Lord speak to her very clearly. He said, "You take care of the sowing and I will bring the increase and the reaping." The lesson was very profound. We serve the Lord of the harvest and we can trust Him with the impossibilities. The timing is in His hands.

Our part in intercession is sowing so that the Lord can bring in the harvest. What an encouragement this story was to me and I pray it is to you too. Sometimes we become despondent thinking nothing is happening but that isn't true. Our God is working His purposes out.

About the Author

Fiona Horrobin is married to Peter, the founder of Ellel Ministries. Between them, they have four married children and nine grandchildren. Fiona has pioneered the work of Ellel Ministries alongside Peter and has over thirty years' experience teaching and praying for people from a wide range of backgrounds and across many nations. She has taught on many different aspects of the healing ministry.

It was through ministering to the broken-hearted that Fiona discovered the keys to healing that flowed out of creative expression. Through discovering their creativity, people were getting deeply in touch with their Creator and experiencing His healing love.

Fiona's passion for seeing God heal the hurting and seeing their lives restored then led her to pioneer the vision for Healing Through Creativity courses within the work of Ellel Ministries. The lessons learned have proved dynamic and relevant to people from every culture and all the nations – from China to Africa and Australia to North America and especially including the formerly devastated nations of Eastern Europe. It was through this work that Fiona also had a personal breakthrough in her own life and discovered her talent for art and painting. Her first book on Healing and Intercession was also the fruit of many years of practical experience of seeing God at work bringing healing and restoration to people's lives.

Ellel Ministries
International

Our Vision

Ellel Ministries is a non-denominational Christian Mission Organization with a vision to resource and equip the Church by welcoming people, teaching them about the Kingdom of God and healing those in need (Luke 9:11).

Our Mission

Our mission is to fulfil the above vision throughout the world, as God opens the doors, in accordance with the Great Commission of Jesus and the calling of the Church to proclaim the Kingdom of God by preaching the good news, healing the broken-hearted and setting the captives free. We are, therefore, committed to evangelism, healing, deliverance, discipleship and training. The particular scriptures on which our mission is founded are Isaiah 61:1–7; Matthew 28:18–20; Luke 9:1–2; 9:11; Ephesians 4:12; 2 Timothy 2:2.

Our Basis of Faith

God is a Trinity. God the Father loves all people. God the Son, Jesus Christ, is Saviour and Healer, Lord and King. God the Holy Spirit indwells Christians and imparts the dynamic power by which they are enabled to continue Christ's ministry. The Bible is the divinely inspired authority in matters of faith, doctrine and conduct, and is the basis for teaching.

For details about the current worldwide activities of Ellel Ministries International please go to: www.ellel.org

Ellel Ministries International
Ellel Grange
Ellel
Lancaster, LA2 0HN
United Kingdom
Tel (+44) (0)1524 751 651

Other titles in the Truth & Freedom Series

All available in eBook format from all the major eBook readers

Anger
How do you handle it?
Paul & Liz Griffin

Size: 5.5"x8.5"
Pages: 112
ISBN: 9781852404505

Hope & Healing for the Abused
Paul & Liz Griffin

Size: 5.5"x8.5"
Pages: 128
ISBN: 9781852404802

Intercession & Healing
Breaking through with God
Fiona Horrobin

Size: 5.5"x8.5"
Pages: 176
ISBN: 9781852405007

Soul Ties
The unseen bond in relationships
David Cross

Size: 5.5"x8.5"
Pages: 128
ISBN: 9781852404512

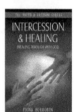

God's Covering
A place of healing
David Cross

Size: 5.5"x8.5"
Pages: 192
ISBN: 9781852404857

The Dangers of Alternative Ways to Healing
How to avoid new age deceptions
David Cross & John Berry

Size: 5.5"x8.5"
Pages: 176
ISBN: 9781852405373

Trapped by Control
How to find freedom
David Cross

Size: 5.5"x8.5"
Pages: 112
ISBN: 9781852405014

Rescue from Rejection
Finding Security in God's Loving Acceptance
Denise Cross

Size: 5.5"x8.5"
Pages: 160
ISBN: 9781852405380

Healing from the consequences of Accident, Shock and Trauma
Peter Horrobin

Size: 5.5"x8.5"
Pages: 168
ISBN: 9781852407438

Stepping Stones to the Father Heart of God
Margaret Silvester

Size: 5.5" x 8.5"
Pages: 176
ISBN: 9781852406233

www.sovereignworld.com

Please visit our online shop to browse our range of titles.
www.sovereignworld.com
or write to the company at the headquarters address:

Sovereign World Ltd.
Ellel Grange
Bay Horse
Lancaster
Lancashire LA2 0HN
United Kingdom

Or email us at:
info@sovereignworld.com

*Most books are also available in e-book format
and can be purchased online.*

Would You Join With Us To Bless the Nations?

At the Sovereign World Trust, our mandate and passion is to send books, like the one you've just read, to *faithful leaders who can equip others* (2 Tim 2:2).

The 'Good News' is that in all of the poorest nations we reach, the Kingdom of God is growing in an accelerated way but, to further this Great Commission work, the Pastors and Leaders in these countries need good teaching resources in order to provide sound Biblical doctrine to their flock, their future generations and especially new converts.

If you could donate a copy of this or other titles from Sovereign World Ltd, you will be helping to supply much-needed resources to Pastors and Leaders in many countries.

Contact us for more information on (+44)(0)1732 851150 or visit our website www.sovereignworldtrust.org.uk

> *"I have all it takes to further my studies. Sovereign is making it all possible for me"*
>
> **Rev. Akfred Keyas – Kenya**

> *"My ministry is rising up gradually since I have been teaching people from these books"*
>
> **Pastor John Obaseki – Nigeria**

Lightning Source UK Ltd.
Milton Keynes UK
UKHW021421161122
412294UK00013B/119